THE BEST FRIEND 2

Maria Marchan

WESTBOW
P R E S S®
A DIVISION OF THOMAS NELSON
& ZONDERVAN

This book is a work of non-fiction. Unless otherwise noted, the author
and the publisher make no explicit guarantees as to the accuracy of
the information contained in this book and in some cases, names
of people and places have been altered to protect their privacy.

Scripture taken from the New King James Version®. Copyright ©
1982 by Thomas Nelson. Used by permission. All rights reserved.

WestBow Press books may be ordered through booksellers or by contacting:

WestBow Press
A Division of Thomas Nelson & Zondervan
1663 Liberty Drive
Bloomington, IN 47403
www.westbowpress.com
1 (866) 928-1240

Because of the dynamic nature of the Internet, any web addresses or
links contained in this book may have changed since publication and
may no longer be valid. The views expressed in this work are solely those
of the author and do not necessarily reflect the views of the publisher,
and the publisher hereby disclaims any responsibility for them.

Any people depicted in stock imagery provided by Getty Images are
models, and such images are being used for illustrative purposes only.
Certain stock imagery © Getty Images.

ISBN: 978-1-9736-1966-6 (sc)
ISBN: 978-1-9736-1965-9 (hc)
ISBN: 978-1-9736-1967-3 (e)

Library of Congress Control Number: 2018901744

Print information available on the last page.

WestBow Press rev. date: 02/27/2018

PREFACE

THE BEST FRIEND 2 is about being the best friend. Just as how you would like your good friend to be sincere toward you, in the same way, you should be genuine to your best friend.

The purpose of The Best Friend 2 is to help you to be the best you can be through God's word and the Holy Spirit. You would learn about the Holy Spirit's role in God's plan for making us into the best we could become. No matter how severe or traumatic your experiences may have been, God is capable and willing to heal and deliver you from them and bringing you to a satisfying and fulfilled life. You just need to be willing to allow God to mold you.

The Best Friend 2 shows the importance of one's relationship with the Lord Jesus Christ and having a strong family life because both are necessary for becoming the best friend. It shows how we can become better people than we are today. Even if a person grew up in a stable home, there would always be room for improvement. The best way to read this book is along with the Bible. Some of the scriptures are as short as one or two verses, and others are a whole chapter. The long scriptures are in parenthesis or brackets. Read the whole Bible chapter along with the paragraph to get the full understanding of what you are reading. In this book, there are examples and illustrations to help you understand clearly.

There was a challenge, which caused a setback in writing this book. I had to deal with some unexpected family matters, so I did not have the time to focus on writing for a little over one year. God is good, and my family situation worked out fine. During that time, I got a wonderful job. When I settled down on my new job, I continued writing until I finished, which turned out fine. I learned more things, which I was able to add to The Best Friend 2.

With the internet, many young people do not read books as often as they should. Instead, they prefer to spend time on social media. Most people use shorthand, like "How r u?", "I will c u 2morrow", and Tks., etc. when they send messages. After some time of continually writing shorthand, someone can forget how to spell and write properly. Therefore, reading helps one to spell properly and learn the meaning of words.

You will notice that the front covers of The Best Friend and The Best Friend 2 are pictures of teenagers of both genders and different races. The reason I chose these pictures is that your best friend does not have to be someone of your gender or race. However, that person should share the same values as you. Look at babies, toddlers, and young children; whether they are rich, middle class or poor, put them together on a playground, and you will notice that they do not "see" the differences in the races or the social status of their friends. Whenever they disagree, they will make up again without any intervention. Even in war, children of opposing sides will play together if they should meet. As children grow up, they learn bad qualities like greed, prejudice, envies, and selfishness from their parents and the adults around them. Do we become less wise and less loving as we grow older than when we were children? Jesus said in Matthew 18:3 "Assuredly, I say to you, unless you are converted and become like little children, you will by no means enter the kingdom of heaven.

Dedication

DEDICATE THIS BOOK TO GERARD, who was sincerely a true friend. He was like my brother after my biological brother died. Leading up to Gerard giving his life to the Lord Jesus Christ, he started reading his Bible. One of Gerard's favorite scripture is from First Corinthians 12:4-11, which is about the gifts of the Holy Spirit. He desired to receive the gift of working of miracles (verse 10). Gerard desired to work miracles among the underprivileged and outcasts in society so they would have a life of dignity and respect.

His desire inspired me to search the scripture about the gifts of the Spirit. I found out from my personal experiences along with studying the Bible that there are many miracles, even in modern times, and nothing is impossible with God. Therefore, Gerard's desire motivated me to reach out to young children from underprivileged conditions and help them to see how Jesus Christ will help them practically. See you in the resurrection, Gerard. You will read about him in Chapter 1.

Precious gemstones go under intense pressure
for them to become as beautiful as they are

CONTENTS

acknowledgment

First Corinthians 15:10 says, "By the grace of God, I am what I am..." All the credit for this book goes to Jesus Christ because of His grace or undeserved favor toward me. By abiding in Jesus Christ, I got the inspiration to write. All praise, glory, and honor belong to Him.

I thank God for giving me a Bible-believing family and relatives who instilled godly values early in my life. They include my maternal grandparents, my parents, and my two favorite aunts, Shirley and Rosemary.

Thanks to my two best friends, Belle and Sylvester. We share the same values, and their continued support encouraged me to write this book. Sylvester even contributed to a portion of the last paragraph in the Preface.

I also thank WestBow Press Publishing, who published my first book, The Best Friend. As it was my first time in writing a book, I was clueless, and they were patient and professional at every step of the process, from the beginning to its completion. WestBow Press Publishing made it easier for me to write this book. WestBow Press Publishing introduced me to the Author Learning Centre, where I got more information from experienced authors about being a successful author through short videos.

I also acknowledge my young Bible students, who motivate me when I see the good results in their lives from the practical application of the Bible. These children are top students in their school. Their parents are proud of them, and people respect them wherever they go.

INTRODUCTION

EQUALLY IMPORTANT IN WISELY SELECTING friends is to be someone else's best friend. We want the best for ourselves, but it would be good if we can be the best friend in someone else's life. It takes a great person to uplift and encourage others. We always see ourselves in the best light and judge others by looking at their flaws. It would be nice for us to see the potential of people overcoming their weaknesses, instead of focusing on their shortcomings. Remember, we also have weaknesses.

In The Best Friend 2, we will consider the problems some people faced in their childhood. The reason for this is that many people had some form of a disadvantage when growing up, which influenced their behavior as adults. We must identify the problem so we would be able to find a solution if we want the matter to turn around and get better. There are Bible and modern day examples and illustrations in The Best Friend 2, which would help you to understand the points.

In chapter 1, you would read about a family's experience of how generational curses can pass down to families and keep them trapped in a dysfunctional state. It goes on to show how their faith in Jesus Christ helped them to break and destroy the curse in their bloodline and overcome their adversities. Gerard, one of the characters in this chapter was my good friend. His sister, Belle, permitted me to write her family's story because it turned out good. Except for Gerard, I changed their names.

Chapter 2 explains why it is futile to blame others and make excuses for one's setback in life. There are examples and illustrations of how blame and excuses affect people negatively and prevent them from being their best.

Chapter 3 explains the true meaning of contentment and its purpose in preparing us to receive our breakthrough.

Chapter 4 is about healing and deliverance from past hurts, especially in childhood. It also goes on to give more details about breaking and destroying generational curses and become the first generation to enjoy the blessings, which you can pass on to future generations. The blessings would make a person become better. There are examples of how it works.

Chapter 5 explains in details Psalm 23, or The Lord is my Shepherd. Many people say this psalm as a prayer. This psalmist wrote this song later on in his life. You will learn three things about Psalm 23, which would make you become a better person. First, to rely on God completely in all situations; second, the purpose of adversities in your life; because the "shadow of the valley of death" experiences are temporary and I will get out of the "valley" victoriously. Third, the Lord will bless you with abundance in every area of your life. It is comforting and practical in showing you how to overcome trials with success.

Chapter 6 is about building our character. It explains how we cultivate and develop godly character through Jesus Christ. The purpose of good character is that we become the best that we can. We must not compare ourselves with others because people should not be our role model, but Jesus Christ.

Chapter 7 is about Jesus Christ, our best friend. You will understand how powerful He is and how He affects us in a great way. There are both Bible and modern day examples of people's lives that Jesus Christ touched.

The modern-day examples in this book are from one family, mentioned in chapter one, and their cousins.

CHAPTER 1

A DYSFUNCTIONAL FAMILY

OU PUT DOWN THE FOUNDATION before the construction of a house begins. The purpose of the foundation is to hold up the house for decades. The house will stand up strong if the foundation is according to the building code. On the other hand, if the foundation is faulty by using inferior materials, no matter how attractive the building is, it will eventually crack up and fall. This same principle applies to human beings. Parents and primary caregivers should build a solid foundation for their children.

Before a contractor lays the foundation for a house, he makes a plan. We do not have to guess about the plan for our lives because God gave it to us. Genesis 1:26-28 when He said, "Then God said, "Let Us make man in Our image, according to Our likeness...." Therefore, God created man in His image; in the image of God He created him; male and female He created them. Then God blessed them, and God said to them, "Be fruitful and multiply; fill the earth and subdue it; have dominion over the fish of the sea, over the birds of the air, and over every living thing that moves on the earth." Before conception, God planned our lives. He is the architect of our lives, so if we follow

Him, we will not live from crisis to crisis; instead, we will live life by God's design.

"Begin Before Birth, What Happens in the Womb can last a Life Time," says about the fetus, that the unborn baby can taste from the tenth week of pregnancy, and he begins to move his eyes during the fourteenth week. The fetus begins to respond to sounds at about twenty weeks into the pregnancy. Around the twenty-sixth week, the fetus feels, touch and feel pain. These early experiences, coupled with our inherited genes, form a lasting impression. From conception until about five to seven years old are the foundational years. These impressions create who the child will grow up to become, and it goes deeper than the mental and emotional state, into the spirit of the person.

Young children's minds take in everything they see and hear, and it stays with them for life. Genes from the parents and the environment in which they live mold the child, from infancy, which begins in the womb. Parents, grandparents, relatives, friends, babysitters, neighbors, the internet, and television shows are the major factors in forming that impression in them. Parents are the primary caregivers and are responsible for creating the environment for their children by deciding whom they allow into their lives.

What parents say and do to their children will also have an impact on their young lives. Psalm 127:3-4 "Children are a heritage from the LORD, and the fruit of the womb is His reward. Like arrows in the hand of a warrior, so are the children of one's youth." Heritage is a valued thing that a previous generation passes down to their descendants. What heritage are you passing down to your children?" Parents have the God-given right to prepare a heritage of high values to give to their young ones. The fruit of the womb is God's reward to you. A reward is something you receive for an achievement. Your babies are the rewards you receive for being loving and responsible parents. Arrows in the hands of a warrior were skilled fighters, so when they shot their arrows, their aim was right on target. Just as the warrior, skilled parents will instill godly values into their infants by following the Word of God, which will stay with them for life. Proverbs 22:6 "Train up a child in the way he should go, and when he is old he will not depart from it." Cherish your precious gift.

The baby is not too young to learn anything because he is taking in everything around him, whether they are good or bad. Parents need to take their responsibility seriously and aim their children in the right direction they would like them to go in life. Do not allow anyone else to direct your children because if you do not guide them someone else would do it for you. For example, parents should teach their children about virtues like godliness, love, kindness, compassion, respect, truthfulness, and honesty, etc. More importantly, teach your children by setting good examples for them to imitate. These children will grow up to be stable and, therefore, they will make wise choices and be successful.

The most common forms of abuse are physical or sexual, but it can also be verbal and emotional, as in the case of the family you are about to read. Many families face abuse in one form or another, and it is responsible for most of the problems in our society. Abused children, who do not get help, grow up with serious defects, and they are unable to function properly. This book shows how abuse makes people dysfunctional until they give their lives to the Lord Jesus Christ, where they can get out of an unstable situation. Therefore, there is hope for those who believe in Jesus Christ.

The following example will show the extent of damage that happens to abused children. Ralph and Frances' family was full of verbal and emotional abuse. Their son, Gerard, was the only son and second child of four children. When they were children, his oldest sister, Belle, who was three years older than he was, was his role model and his two younger sisters, Becky and Danella used to do everything he did, including wearing shorts and jerseys like him. They used to ride their tricycles and play ball games together. Everything seemed normal about these four children, but they were not. Every day these children were verbally and emotionally abused, especially Gerard. Gerard's father belittled him almost every day. To understand what happened to Gerard and his sisters, let us first understand the background of their parents.

The parents of Belle, Gerard, Becky, and Danella also came from abusive homes. Belle's father Ralph was born in 1931, and he was the eighth child from a family of fifteen children. These children were between fifteen and eighteen months apart from each other. Ralph's father was a farmer, and he worked very hard, from daybreak until sunset, so he could have sold his produce to provide for his rapidly growing family. As a child, Ralph was bright and at the top of his class in English, arithmetic (math), and geography. This incident took place back in the 1930s in a developing country, and primary school level of education was available to all, but not secondary school. In those days, the majority of families was poor and could not afford to pay for secondary schooling. If a child was very bright, he might get a scholarship to go to high school. Ralph's teachers were impressed with his schoolwork, and they would tell his parents that he had a good chance of getting a scholarship. His father was proud of him because nobody in his family had completed primary school, much more to go to high school before.

On the other hand, Ralph's mother was illiterate because she did not go to school, and she was jealous of him because nobody said anything good about her other children who showed little interest in studying. Whenever she saw Ralph studying at home, she would snap at him with insults. She used to make derogatory remarks about him to his siblings, and in turn, they would ridicule him. Ralph's family would put him down in public with him being present. They would say, "Ralph is a lazy boy," "he is wicked" and "he is a good-for-nothing." Even the neighbors would insult him and call him "a bad boy." He felt bad about himself all the time. He preferred to spend time alone with the animals, as they could not talk.

Ralph's mother would cook chicken from the yard because the poorer people could not afford to buy chicken and eggs, so they reared them, along with other small animals like ducks, turkeys, and goats. They did not have electricity in their home; therefore, they did not own a refrigerator. Ralph's mother prepared curry goat one Sunday in the month and invited relatives over on that day. Ralph's duties included assisting his mother by putting the cutlery on the table. When everyone had eaten, he would wash the dishes and then eat. There was no chair for Ralph, so he would sit on the floor and look on. He was a child when the bad treatment from his mother began. From the age of six years old, Ralph's mother would wake him up at four o'clock every morning to tend to the poultry before having breakfast to go to school. By the time he was eight years old, he had begun to care for the goats. During the week when his mother had prepared meals for her family, she would make Ralph watch his siblings eat food with chicken or duck, and like any child, he felt rejected and hurt. When they were finished eating, she would put all the leftover food on a plate and give it to Ralph. If he wanted to eat a proper lunch with chicken in it, he used to kill a chicken and cook it for himself or wait until Sunday when his father was at home, and he would give Ralph chicken breast. The bad treatment Ralph faced, began to take place when he was under the age of ten. From the age of six years old, Ralph learned to do many things that his mother should have done for him, like cooking and cleaning. Back then, many people cooked outside on a fireside, which they made of mud and wood. To cook the food, they would put the pot on the wood, which was in the clay mold, and light it. Ralph also started to iron his school clothes when he was eight years old. In those days, someone would put the iron on the outdoor fireside, and then iron the clothes. Cooking on the outdoor fireside was dangerous for a child.

One of Ralph's teachers gave him a guitar as a gift for being a bright boy to encourage him. The demeaning treatment from his mother made Ralph an angry boy, and he used to channel his anger into playing the guitar in the chicken house where he had some peace of mind. Ralph's studies and his love for the guitar aggravated his mother even more. Ralph's father had a soft spot for him because he knew of the abuse his son was undergoing, but because of the long hours of work, he was away from home most of the time. He also would have liked to send his son to secondary school, but just could not have afforded it, so he hoped his son would get a scholarship. Ralph's mother and siblings would not include him in their activities, so he continued his studies or played his guitar because this is where he found peace of mind. Many families face abuse in one form or another, and it is responsible for most of the problems in our society. Abused children, who do not get help, grow up with serious defects, and they are unable to function properly.

Children thrive on the acceptance, approval, and acknowledgment from their parents. Twice in the Bible, our Heavenly Father acknowledged and approved of Jesus as His beloved Son. The first time was at his baptism at the Jordan River before He went into His ministry and the second time was at the mount of transfiguration. (Matthew 3:17; 17:5) Jesus came from heaven, and He created everything in the whole universe, from the smallest atom to the biggest star, yet God found it necessary to acknowledge and approve of Him, or it would not have been in the Bible for us to read. Everything written in the Bible is for our benefit. Parents could learn something from this event.

Ralph did not get the scholarship he desired because his mother took him out of school six months before his exams at the age of twelve. She sent him to live with his two older brothers, who got jobs in the city, which was thirty-four miles away from home. Ralph became resentful, as he had to cook meals and do housekeeping for his brothers. He was angry because he wanted to go to high school and his family took the opportunity away from him. Ralph got his first job at fifteen years old. The first thing he bought for himself was a Bible from an ex-priest. Back then, the clergy of the church did not permit the common people to read their Bibles, so Ralph hid it in the hen house at his parents' home and hardly ever read it, and then he forgot about it until many years later. Even though he lived with his brothers, he would send half of his salary at home to help, but his mother was never satisfied with whatever he contributed. He wanted to please her to the point that he would go out of his way to do nice things for her. She would repeatedly hurl sarcastic remarks at him. Ralph felt that his father should have intervened, but he did not. He started to think that his parents hated him because they had adopted him, even though he resembled his mother. If Ralph grew up in modern times, the authorities would have taken him away from home for child abuse and press charges against his parents.

After one year of working, Ralph left his brothers and went to live on his own. He became friendly with some older men who used to smoke cigarettes and go to the bars. Of course, it was not long after his new friends introduced him to cigarette smoking and eventually alcohol. Ralph could not keep a job for long because the combination of rage and alcohol got him into trouble with his work. After many years, he met a lovely girl named Frances, and they got married.

Frances was born ten years after Ralph to a working-class family in 1941. That means they lived comfortably with electricity and indoor plumbing and their parents were able to pay their daughters' tuition to go to high school. As a child, her father was a railway master and a hard worker, and her mother was a homemaker. Frances was the second child of four girls.

Frances' father used to leave early in the morning to go to work and return late in the evening. Early on mornings, from Monday to Friday, after her husband left for work, Frances' mother, named Delores, would leave her four young daughters at home alone to go to church, then she would visit the local soothsayers. The soothsayers used to give Delores disturbing information about her husband and her neighbors so she would continue to visit them. On one occasion, the soothsayers told her that her husband was building a house for the woman across the road. Delores put a tablespoon of a dried herb, which she got from one soothsayer, into her husband's food so he would remain faithful to her. He got so sick that he sweated profusely, so Delores thought he was dying and had to take him to the hospital. Later on, the doctors told her that the herb he had ingested was what the wild animals in the forests ate for cleansing, but it was unsuitable for human consumption. Frances and her older sister, Margaret, used to sit with their father to make the monthly budget with his modest salary, so he could not have afforded to build a house for anyone else.

The soothsayers told Delores that her neighbors were jealous of her because her house had electricity and indoor plumbing and she had beautiful furnishings. Her neighbors' 'jealousy' made Delores suspicious of their every move. The neighbors next door would be laughing among themselves, and she would feel they were laughing at her. If someone had visitors, she felt they were talking about her business. Delores even verbally accused her neighbors of being jealous of her, and they would laugh at her. Another time she accused one of her neighbors of stealing her pot of stew beef, but it was her mischievous eldest daughter, Margaret, who ate the beef and shared it with Frances, Rosanne, and Amoy, her three younger sisters. The soothsayers used to make potions from various herbs for all types of problems and sell to Delores. At six o'clock every evening, she would walk around her house, sprinkling potion to keep evil spirits away from her family. Back then in the 1940s, entertainment was limited to the working class, so the neighbors would sit on their porches to look at Delores while she sprinkled the potion and laughed at her. She was the joke of the neighborhood.

Delores even went as far as to take her daughters along with her to one of her visits. It was a scary experience for these young girls. The soothsayer frightened their mother by saying the neighbors put evil spirits on her daughters because they were bright and pretty girls. Her neighbors wanted to prevent her children from progressing. The soothsayer said these things in the presence of the girls. To get rid of the evil spirits the soothsayer prepared baths with lime juice, salt and a potion made with some herbs for the children to bathe. These are a few of the weird instructions from the soothsayers Delores used to follow. No right thinking parent would subject his or her children to anything horrendous like that, but then Delores was not thinking right.

These abnormal events took place when Frances and her sisters were under the age of ten. Margaret used to prepare breakfast and dress her sisters for school because Delores would leave early to visit her "people," as she called the soothsayers. Delores should have stayed at home to dress her daughters for school. They did not know about personal hygiene, so their clothes were unkempt, and their heads were full of dandruff. Margaret tried her best to comb their tangled hair because it was long, thick and wavy, so she was unable to manage. The best way to comb their hair was to put coconut oil in their hair and then brush the top of their hair and tried to put two braids each, which were uneven. Margaret would give her sisters and herself cod liver oil, which fell on their school uniform most of the time. Rancid cod liver oil on clothes and coconut oil on hair smelt awful during the heat of the day in a tropical country. Instead of the teachers helping these young girls by speaking to their father about his daughters' condition, they used to ridicule them and incited the other children in the class to tease and laugh at them. Back then, teachers did not know about the negative impact verbal and mental abuse had on children.

Frances' father was a good provider for his family, but he used to put his daughters down. On one occasion, his eldest daughter, Margaret played one of the three wise men in a Christmas concert. Her father told her that the other two wise men played the part better than she did. That remark hurt Margaret deeply. Frances was an A student in high school. In her final exams in high school, she got high grades in all her subjects and three credits. Instead of her father congratulate his daughter for doing well; he scolded her for not getting distinctions as his colleague's daughter. Those words broke Frances' confidence as she studied diligently to pass her exams. Her father would criticize his daughters by comparing them with other children. Rosanne and Amoy were good at playing the piano. Both of them wanted to become piano teachers, but their father would say to them, "Who do you all think you are?" "Other children are better than you. Nobody in our family ever reached so far!" These remarks broke Roseanne and Amoy's hearts and their enthusiasm to pursue their career in music diminished. He did not realize that by comparing his daughters to others, he was destroying their self-worth.

When a child hears his parents compare him to other children, it breaks his zeal and determination to keep on going. Each child is an individual with unique talents. One child may be good at math while another is good at creative writing, so the comparison is unfair. Frances' father did not realize that other families had their problems, but no one knows what goes on behind closed doors.

Delores' relatives and people in their neighborhood used to call Delores a witch. If this had happened in our time, the authorities would have taken these children away from their parents. Delores's wacky behavior embarrassed Frances, her sisters and their father. Children would tease these four girls about their crazy mother. Therefore, Frances and her four sisters grew up always feeling bad. The only fun they had was when Margaret made mischief at home and blamed one of the neighbors, and this would cause their mother to accuse one of the neighbors, which would have become a quarrel. These quarrels were another reason for the neighbors to laugh.

These four girls learned to be tidy and neat by the time they were teenagers. Although Frances and her sisters were bright academically, they completed high school and got good jobs they had low self-worth, which caused them to make bad choices in their relationships. They felt as if they did not deserve the best, even when they wished for better things in life. Then Frances met Ralph, and they got married.

When two dysfunctional people get married, that is a recipe for serious problems. Frances worked as a secretary in a small private Company in the early 1960s. During that time she met Ralph, and they got married one and a half year later. Even though Frances thought that Ralph was ill-bred, she felt that any well-mannered young man would not show interest in her. Therefore, it would be better to accept Ralph's marriage proposal, or she might have remained a spinster.

Shortly after getting married, Frances realized that she had to support the family, as her new husband lost his job. When Frances was pregnant with her children, there were times when she did not feel well and would have liked to stay at home, but she had to work to take care of her growing family. Those times were very stressful for her. Remember, babies in the womb take in everything on the outside. Those babies were receiving stress from Frances. Ralph and Frances had four children, Belle, Gerard, Becky, and Danella.

No one wanted to hire Ralph anymore, as his employers fired him for his unreliability and his unpredictable outbursts. He was very insecure, and he took out his frustration on his wife and children. Ralph would snap at any man for looking at his young wife and then blame her. He would shout at Frances and make remarks like, "You are encouraging the men to look at you! You do like their admiring glances toward you! Have you forgotten that you have a husband?" He used to curse his family when he was drunk, even Delores. Ralph and Delores were at loggerheads frequently.

Ralph would put down Gerard in the worst manner, both in the privacy of the home as well as in public among his peers. The insults and outbursts against Gerard began when he was still a baby while learning to walk. Ralph would shout at his baby son and say things like, "You are a stupid boy! Walk, you idiot!" or if he spilled milk or water, Ralph would shout, "You are a clumsy fool!" He did not hit him, but his words felt like sharp knives, as he hurled these types of outbursts at him over the years. Gerard did not have any friends because he did not know how to be friendly so he could not fit in anywhere. The cruel things his father would say to him in public embarrassed him. His mother, sisters and one of his close cousins were the only people he knew how to relate. His classmates did not understand him and thought he was strange, so they did not play with him.

Iyanla Vanzant, in her book "Peace from Broken Pieces," said, "How parents deal with their children creates a direct line of the things they need to heal themselves." Ralph wanted his only son to be the best, but he did not know how to bring out the best in him. Ralph knew that he needed healing from his childhood hurts, but he did not know how. He knew that his behavior was wrong, but he could not help himself. Although Gerard got most of the abuse, it affected his sisters, which gave them the fear of people in authority, like teachers, police officers, and most adults. Therefore, they were timid girls, and they did not know how to express themselves, so they did not. They were always concerned about not to offend anyone at the cost of their peace of mind.

Ralph's wife, his parents, in-laws, and acquaintances (he did not have any friends) did not know what to do, except to pray, which was the best thing. Although he bought a Bible, thirty-two years ago, he did not read it after hiding it in his parents' hen house. By the late 1970s, Ralph's doctors diagnosed him with a mental disorder, which was the reason for his frequent outbursts of anger. Ralph decided that it was time to start reading his Bible, so he went to his parents' home to get it from the place where the chicken house used to be. He had taken it out of the wrapped newspaper and plastic bag and took it home to read.

When Belle was twelve years old, she got a Good News Bible as a birthday gift. Times had changed, and there were some modern versions of the Bible. By this time, the clergy allowed its members to read Bibles, and Belle realized that she had a strong desire to read the Bible. She felt as if her copy of the Bible had a magnet and it was drawing her to read. She knew that her family had been praying for years so that her father will change his bad ways, but nothing seemed to be working. Ralph had started reading his Bible, but he was still an alcoholic, smoking cigarettes, jobless, and insulting and belittling his family. Although Belle's family used to pray and go to church, they did not read the Bible regularly. Belle's grandparents used to read the psalms, proverbs, and some accounts from the Gospels from the time she was a baby until she got her personal Bible. Therefore, she was familiar with some scripture.

Belle wondered why God was not answering their prayers. What Belle did not know at that time, is that the strong desire to read the Bible did not happen by chance. It was the answer to the prayers of the adults in her family over the years. We do not know how God will answer our prayers. She began by reading the Gospels and Acts of the Apostles, and Psalms and Proverbs, as she was familiar with them. These scriptures stirred up something inside of her she never felt before, which she later learned was the power of the Holy Spirit. She would also listen to televangelists, and they would explain the scripture. As a minor, she could not just visit a church without her parents' permission. This time was in the late 1970s, and those days, young people were still willingly obedient to their parents. Nevertheless, Belle gave her life to the Lord when she was fourteen years old. By this time, she had started reading the rest of the New Testament, and then she began reading parts of the Old Testament.

Belle began to share the scripture first with her siblings and then with her parents. Her two sisters accepted the Lord into their lives shortly after. A year later, her mother gave her life to the Lord. By this time, they were attending a Bible-believing church, they began to understand scripture clearly, and they began to pray according to the Word of God. They also began to realize that the words in the Bible are very powerful. In the meantime,

Ralph continued to be an alcoholic, a heavy smoker, jobless, and verbally abusive toward his wife and children, especially Gerard. Gerard is now a young man, he is resentful toward his father, and he is equally verbally abusive toward him.

The women of this family were persistent in their Bible reading and prayer. Their prayer was different from the past. Now, they understood Scripture like Luke 10:18-19 where Jesus said, "I saw Satan fall like lightning from heaven. Behold, I give you the authority to trample on serpents and scorpions, and over all the power of the enemy, and nothing shall by any means hurt you." "Serpents and scorpions" represents the devil and his demons. "All the power of the enemy" means that Satan has power, but his power is limited because he is a created being. "Nothing shall by any means hurt you," means that Satan and his demons cannot hurt us when we are under the authority of Jesus Christ. The authority that Jesus gives is to stand in His name. The devil's power is no match for Jesus' power.

Belle, her sisters and her mother took hold of the authority that Jesus Christ gave them in His name to speak to circumstances, and they began to see results. Their prayers went something like this, "We address the spirits of addiction, mental disorder, and rage. We command you to leave Ralph/father for good and never return in the name of Jesus Christ." Also, Isaiah 54:17 "No weapon formed against our family shall prosper, and every tongue which rises against us in judgment You shall condemn. This is the heritage of the servants of the LORD, and their righteousness is from Me," says the LORD." "We take the authority in the name of Jesus Christ and declare that the weapons of childhood hurts and mental disorder, be destroyed by the roots and be replaced with the soundness of mind and peace." They would continue to speak to the addictions and hurts of the past and command them to leave their loved one in the name of Jesus Christ.

Then one day, sometime early in 1982, Ralph could not stand the smell of the alcohol, as he got nauseous whenever he smelled it. After a few failed attempts to have a drink, he realized that he lost the taste to drink alcohol, and he never drank again. About four months' later, he started coughing when he lit the cigarette to smoke; then he also realized that he had lost the taste for smoking too, and he never smoked again. He also developed a stronger desire to read and meditate on the Bible. He also wanted to be a good husband and a good father. Ralph gave his life to the Lord Jesus Christ, and he got baptized in water. Weekly church attendance was regular. Bible discussion and prayer was the family devotion on evenings and had become a normal part of their daily lives. Ralph's behavior gradually began to mellow down. In time, people in his neighborhood started calling him the Bible preacher, because he enjoyed sharing scripture with them. Family life was settling down fine, except for one person – Gerard.

Gerard was a very angry and bitter young man. He did not want to have anything to do with his father, so he kept away from family worship. The doctors diagnosed Gerard as having a mental disorder too, like his father, which explained his behavior. Sometimes he would isolate himself from everyone, including his family, and at other times, there would be verbal outbursts, mainly toward his father. He displayed all his father's traits, except for the drinking and smoking. It felt as if the problem had started all over again. In the late 1980s, counseling was not prevalent as it is today.

Gerard's family would regularly pray for him. His big sister, Belle, used to read regularly and explain the scripture to him. She would explain the meaning of John 3:16 "For God so loved the world that He gave His only begotten Son, that whoever believes in Him should not perish but have everlasting life."

Romans 5:9-10 "Much more then, having now been justified by His blood, we shall be saved from wrath through Him. For if when we were enemies we were reconciled to God through the death of His Son, much more, having been reconciled, we shall be saved by His life." She would also show him Colossians 3:13 bearing with one another, and forgiving one another if anyone has a complaint against another; even as Christ forgave you, so you also must do." She told him that when he forgives his father, then his deliverance would come. In April of 1990, Gerard announced to his family that he wanted to give his life to the Lord, and he started going to church. He told his pastor that he wanted him to baptize him, which took place three months later in mid-July. Gerard's family was happy to see the whole family saved. Tragedy struck shortly after and rocked the new life that this family was building through Jesus Christ.

Late in October of that year, Gerard felt sick. He could not eat nor drink, not even water. His family took him to the hospital, only to get the horrifying news that his kidneys were deteriorating fast and he did not have a long time to live. He died five days later. That was a big shock for his loved ones. Questions went through their minds like, "Why did God let this happen to us?" "We are saved by the grace of our Lord Jesus Christ. Did we do something wrong?" "How could the devil attack us so harshly?" They grieved severely. Parents should not have to prepare a funeral for their children; it is the other way around. Belle got nightmares for months that demons were trying to suffocate her, so her aunt Margaret decided to sleep in the same room with her. The bad dreams were surely an attack from the devil to sabotage their newfound faith and to make them believe that God had abandoned them.

Ralph and Frances' family know the Bible account of the death and resurrection of Jesus' good friend Lazarus, recorded in John 11. Gerard did not get a resurrection like Lazarus, but their consolation is in Jesus words to Martha at verse 25, "Jesus said to her, "I am the resurrection and the life. He who believes in Me, though he may die, he shall live." (Read Acts 24:15; 1 Corinthians 15:20-22) Resurrection is coming! If the Bible says so, then it will happen because Isaiah 55:11 reads, "So shall My word be that goes forth from My mouth; It shall not return to Me void, But it shall accomplish what I please, and it shall prosper in the thing for which I sent it." The resurrection is a time in the future when Jesus Christ will raise the dead. (John 5:28-29) Those who died in Christ will receive a glorified body to be with the King of kings and the Lord of lords, Jesus Christ. (First Thessalonians 4:13-18) Belle and her family have the hope of the resurrection that they would meet Gerard again as well as all their loved ones who had passed on but without sickness and problems. This family went through the process of their grief trusting God for comfort.

Belle and her family learned that there are times when life will push you into the fire or throw you into to floodwater with the intention to destroy you. Isaiah 43:2 "When you pass through the waters, I will be with you; and through the rivers, they shall not overflow you. When you walk through the fire, you shall not be burned, nor shall the flame scorch you." They found out that the fire cannot burn them and the floodwater cannot drown them because of Jesus Christ as their Savior. Instead, He would make you walk on water as He did. (Matthew 14:29)

In time, Belle's family overcame the grief of Gerard's death. They remember him today with fondness. They regularly continued to worship God and have family devotion every evening. Continuous family devotion also prepared them to deal with vicious attacks from the devil and his demons in the future, who tried to undermine their relationship with the Lord and destroy their reputation, especially Belle and her sisters. It also helped them to handle the deaths of Ralph and Frances' parents and some other family members in the future. With the help of the Lord Jesus Christ, they overcame every adverse situation they faced. Today, they are successful, and they use their experiences and knowledge to help many to overcome generational curses in their families and replace them with blessings through the Lord Jesus Christ.

Ralph and Frances' family shows us that the previous generation had problems, which they passed down to their descendants. Although both of their fathers were hard workers and good providers for their families, they were also weak men. They did not know how to deal with the situations that arose because of their unstable wives, which distressed their children. We will not judge them because they had problems of their own and they did not know how to deal with them. If we go back to two or three generations before these events took place, most likely we would see that they too had serious problems.

Belle's determination to persevere in the Lord is to be the first generation, along with her parents and sisters, to break and destroy the mental disorders in their family and bad traits like emotional and verbal abuse, lack, and addictions in her family line. She desires to begin afresh with new habits, which in turn will become a new lifestyle to pass down to future generations, which are generational blessings through the Lord Jesus Christ.

The following chapters will show how Belle and her family grew. They are still growing because as long as we are living, we are getting a fresh understanding of our Lord Jesus Christ.

CHAPTER 2

BLAME AND EXCUSES

BLAMING BEGAN IN THE GARDEN of Eden. When God confronted Adam after he ate the fruit from the tree of knowledge of good and evil, he blamed Eve and then God. Adam said, "The woman whom You gave to be with me, she gave me of the tree, and I ate." When God confronted Eve, she blamed the serpent and said, "The serpent deceived me, and I ate." (Genesis 3:12-13). The problem with blaming others is that the situation remains the same, and in many instances, they get worse. In the case of Adam and Eve, we are experiencing the consequences of their wrong deed today because they passed it down to all humankind. People must take responsibility for their actions. We need a solution to the problem and blaming hinders it.

The family mentioned in the previous chapter could have blamed God for the death of Gerard, and they could have blamed Ralph for not being a good husband and father. They could have even blamed their mother Frances for staying in a bad marriage, which affected the children. Ralph and Frances could have blamed their parents for not being good to them. Each generation could blame the generation before them and where would the blaming have gotten them? Nowhere, instead, they would have continuously complained about their situation, which would have made them miserable. Questions did arise, like, "Why did this happen to me?", "I did my best, but what went wrong?", And "Is God punishing me?" Bad things happen in life sometimes, so we trust God to help us in these trying times. God does not cause bad things to happen, but we live in a fallen world, and trials and tribulations are a part of it. Some people think that God should have stopped Adam and Eve from listening to the devil in the Garden of Eden. If God had done that, then He would have taken away man's freedom of choice. God cannot go back on His word. That means He would have contradicted Himself when He said, "Let us make man in our image and likeness." God has freedom of choice, and since He made us in His image and likeness, then we have freedom of choice. Adam and Eve are responsible for the problems of humankind. (Genesis 3:1-7) God provided a solution to the bad situation in which we are.

Grief is normal with the death of a loved one or the experience of any distress. However, the pain goes through a process and then it will be over. On the other hand, prolonged grief, which goes on for many years, even decades, is abnormal, and the person develops a victim mentality. Thus, he remains one, which is evident by his continuous bitterness, animosity, and negative qualities. Harboring animosity toward those who caused the hurt does not solve it. Instead, it makes the bad situation worse, and the individual hurts himself repeatedly.

As Christians, we should support each other while going through trying times, out of compassion for our fellow man. (Romans 12:15) Do not minimize the effects of the bad experiences because they were real and had deep-rooted emotional, mental, and sometimes physical wounds. Proverbs 14:10 said, "The heart knows its bitterness." One person should not judge another because he does not know all the facts or the details of the painful experiences of someone else. God is the only One who can see our hearts and knows all the facts. Each one reacts to adversities and processes them differently because we are all unique individuals. It is easy to tell another person what he should or should not do in a situation, but you are not him, and you are not in his position. For example, Belle, Becky, and Danella are sisters, yet they responded differently to the problems in their home. Belle rarely visited her friends' homes because she did not want to reciprocate the invitation, as she was embarrassed to invite her classmates to her home in case her father was drunk. Another reason is that her strange grandmother might have said something out of context, which can be funny to her listeners, but annoying to Belle. She used to pretend to fit in with her peers, but she did not fit in. She felt as if she could not connect with her friends. Becky could not focus on her studies at school as she was worried about how hard her mother had to work and her father did not appreciate her. The disturbing environment had Danella stressed out to the point that she had an overactive bladder until she was eleven years old and, as she became a teenager, her peers shrugged her off. There were times when she overheard her classmates talking behind her back about her frequent use of the washroom and that she was a sad girl. Gerard, the brother of these three sisters, was timid. He had no friends because he was afraid and he did not know how to interact with anyone. At school, Gerard did not play with his classmates, as he preferred to stay by himself. All four children displayed some form of defect in their personalities.

Nevertheless, as bad as it may be, the effects of bad experiences should not keep anyone stuck in the past. When that person continuously complains about his problem, year after year, about his childhood abuse or the injustice toward him, he keeps reliving the hurt. Even if someone offered advice, the individual would not listen as he is looking for people to agree with him in his plight and join in his misery. This amount of complaining is too much for anyone to carry for this length of time and it becomes poisonous to his health and his relationships, and then he continues to blame people for treating him badly. Do not complain about what you cannot change. The past has gone, and we cannot bring it back. If you repeatedly talk about your hurts, it will become your identity, which is a victim. People avoid a complaining person because it becomes annoying to his listeners and is very draining. We have no control over what others said or did in the past, but we have control over what we decide to do with our lives today. Disgruntled people should take responsibility and do something about their hurts. Besides prayer, hurting people can seek professional counseling, which would help them recover.

To remain a victim of circumstances takes too much out of you and it will make you sick. These experiences can paralyze a person to the point that keeps him back from progressing in life because it is like putting salt on a wound, which would irritate the injury and prevent it from healing. How you see yourself is the same way others will see you and treat you accordingly. Your demeanor reflects your perception of yourself – by the image you portray and the way you behave. Therefore, if you see yourself as a victim, then others will also see and treat you as a victim. For instance, there was a time when Ralph felt he was worthless and people said he was a worthless man.

There are two types of victims; those who seem to be successful by achieving their career goals, yet they repeatedly make bad decisions and have some bad traits as dishonesty, envy, faultfinding, malice, harmful gossiping, backstabbing, or insecurities, etc. They may not even be able to keep healthy relationships. Others may even have bad habits, like substance abuse, smoking, gambling, and immorality. Their career life may be successful, but their personal life is crashing. Then there are those who do not accomplish anything, and they do not have the enthusiasm or the zeal to push forward in life. These people live as if they are in a trance because they are unable to focus.

A victim mentality keeps these individuals in a prison of misery. They feel trapped and hate how their lives are a continuous mishap, but they do not know what to do to get out of their heartache. Therefore, they accept it as their lot in life and may even see themselves as being unlucky. Luck has nothing to do with a person's outcome in life; it is a choice. If you choose to remain a victim of your past, then you will continue to be miserable. On the other hand, if you choose to release your past, then you will become free to enjoy your life. We are free to choose the direction we want our lives to go. Deuteronomy 11:26-28, "Behold, I set before you today a blessing and a curse: the blessing, if you obey the commandments of the LORD your God which I command you today and the curse, if you do not obey the commandments of the LORD your God." Those with a victim mentality will continue to blame their past, the present, the young generation, the older generation, their employer, their peers, the government, the economy, and whomever else they can blame.

Some people did not have a proper childhood. No one chose their parents and the kind of people they were and the neighborhood in which they grew up but, as an adult, you can change whatever went wrong when you were a child because now you have a choice. Some of what we experienced from our parents or guardians were bad and gave us an inferiority complex. We should be aware that parents are not perfect and they too made mistakes when they were younger. Some of these mistakes overflowed into their children's lives, as they had to deal with their deficiencies while taking care of their children. Blaming a bad childhood for one's setbacks and struggles would keep that individual stuck in discouragement and dismay, which would be a hindrance from moving forward.

Ralph's family shows us that the cycle of abuse will continue from generation to generation until Jesus Christ destroys it. Most likely, Ralph's mother was a victim of abuse when she was a child, and she took it out on him. There could have been a few reasons why she picked on him. One possibility is that Ralph was a bright student, and she did not get the opportunity to go to school as he did, so she was jealous. Maybe she also had a mental illness, or it could be that she was resentful that her husband was very proud of his son, and nobody was proud of her. Whatever the reason, it affected Ralph to the point that he also abused his family. Even though Ralph's father felt sorry for his son, he never addressed the matter because he did not know how to handle the bad situation. We do not have all the facts of what he went through as a child, but he came from a tumultuous home. Maybe, he did not know how to deal with the verbal outbursts from his wife. Regardless of what happened to his parents, Ralph felt alone and helpless for a long time.

Frances also came from a dysfunctional home without proper guidance. Her mother, Delores, was not even aware that her eccentric behavior was embarrassing to her family. It is possible that she had a mental illness; no one knows. On the other hand, Frances' father grew up in the orphan home without love and acceptance. His charges met his basic needs of food, clothing, shelter, and primary education, but no warmth or tenderness. He was also a victim of a bully at the orphan home and school. He grew up insecure and had some issues to deal with, so he did not know how to handle the weird situations in which his wife put his family. By comparing his daughters to other children, he was expressing his shortcomings. Nevertheless, Frances and her sisters felt bad whenever he put them down. Frances was naïve and insecure, and she did not know how to deal with alcoholism and verbal outbursts from her husband. Frances had to take the reins as the sole breadwinner for her family, including her husband who could not keep a job. Like Ralph, she also carried her childhood experiences into her adult life. Frances grew up feeling embarrassed most of the time because of her mother's behavior. As an adult, she had a husband who also embarrassed her. Her relatives, the neighbors, and colleagues at work had no respect for him, and this made her feel bad, and it also affected their children. Ralph's family developed insecurities and were timid because their home was unstable. With time, they learned how to overcome these obstacles. However, if they had continued to blame their fore parents for their dysfunctional state, they would have remained miserable and make a bad situation worse.

Equal to blaming others is making excuses. Excuses are the reasons people give to justify their wrong actions. A rude person may try to explain his bad manners by saying something like this, "When I was a child, people treated me badly, so this is why I am like this.". "My mannerism is crude because nobody taught me anything else." or "I cannot help myself from stealing because I had very little as a child." No one may have taught you values or good habits, but you are an adult now, so learn from those who are successful. People make numerous excuses for their bad behavior and actions all the time. While others move forward in life, they will stay behind.

An illustration of this is a like a plant that you keep indoors and give it tap water and limited sunlight. Compare it to the one kept in the yard that got natural sunlight and rain. Even though the plant inside your house will grow, it will not flourish as the one on the outside. The psalmist at Psalm 1:3

said about the person who delights himself in the Lord, "He shall be like a tree planted by the rivers of water that bring forth its fruit in its season, whose leaf also shall not wither; and whatever he does shall prosper." The righteous person flourishes like trees by the river, and he will progress while the person with the victim mentality will remain at a standstill. The person who continues to make excuses without even trying to improve his life is like the plant you keep in the house. He is alive because his brain is working and his heart is beating, but he is not enjoying his life. He is unhappy because his sad life consumes him and he is jealous of those who are progressing. He develops negative qualities like envy, malicious gossiping, a critical attitude, and insecurities. This negative attitude locks a person into a gloomy dungeon of misery and sadness. People do not want to be friends with someone who is sour and sulks at everyone and everything, and they avoid him.

Do not use your family background or the unfair treatment you got in the past, as an excuse to remain locked in a dysfunctional state where you blame others and make excuses. It will keep you in a prison of torment for the rest of your life unless you decide to do something about it. The only person who gets hurt is you. Look at this illustration; you are taking a walk in the park, and you trip over a stone and fall. What would you do? Would you stay on the ground and complain to every passerby about the stone that made you fall? They will think you are silly to lie there and wonder, "Why doesn't he get up"? Instead, you will get up and dust yourself off. You will check to see if you got an injury, move on and attend to the wound as soon as possible. You will not be telling people twenty, thirty, and forty years later, about your fall in the park and show them the scar on your elbow or knee. Life is like this; unfair circumstances happen to us. Just as with a physical fall, we will get up, attend to the situation and move on.

Many persons think that by blaming others and making excuses, we exclude ourselves from the problem and throw the responsibility on someone else. Blaming and making excuses are masks, which people use to hide deep hurts. People do not want others to see their pain because they will see their weaknesses. For anyone to know of their limitations, would be embarrassing. Therefore, others must see him as strong and in control of situations. The mask covers the symptoms, but it does not get rid of the source of the problem. To cover the symptoms is like hiding a crack in the floor with a rug. People see the beautiful rug, but they do not know that under it, there is a crack. The crack in the floor means that there might be a problem with the foundation. The crack gets deeper than it was, and then it will weaken the building, and it will eventually fall. We must get to the source of the problem, which is to strengthen the foundation by fixing it, and the same principle applies to our lives. The person with a victim mentality condemns himself. Self-condemnation is like the crack in the floor, and it causes the problem, which we must fix, or we will fall apart. Negative qualities and bad traits are the results of condemning oneself.

CHAPTER 3

CONTENTMENT

IT IS HARD TO TRY to make a miserable person happy because of his negative attitude toward life. He says that he wants to be happy, but it eludes him because he keeps reliving his past hurts and is waiting for the next event or occasion. Therefore, he continues to be despondent. Happiness is short term, for example, Christmas, a birthday, going to parties, a wedding, the birth of a baby, passing exams, a raise in salary, buying a new house, a new car, etc. The entire list above is very good, and they should make us happy, but we do not experience these events on a daily basis. You have fun at a party, but you do not party twenty-four hours a day and seven days a week. That is unrealistic, and you go back to face everyday life. You may have to tolerate a troublesome employer or co-worker, but you cannot just leave your job because you have your commitment. Even if you leave one job for another, you will meet problems there too. We celebrate our birthdays and Christmas once a year. We go to a wedding, probably two or maybe, three times for the year.

How often is a baby born into your family? You will need to feed, bathe, and change the baby. Baby cries and wakes his parents at 2:00 a.m. when the night is cold, and sleep is sweet. Baby grows into a toddler and throws a tantrum if he does not get his way. When the young child begins to go to school, you will need to buy textbooks, school bag, and school uniform, which means more expenses and this, will go on until your child finishes university at the age of about twenty-three years old. You may need to take a second mortgage on the dream house you bought a few years ago to finance your child's tertiary education. We study if we wish to pass our exams. You may have to work overtime on the job since you got a substantial increase in pay. We become familiar with the car and complain about the traffic on the road, the cost of gas went up again, and that car parts are too expensive. These examples show us that happiness wears off after the excitement of the new things or the occasions are over or when we get comfortable. What about the days, weeks, and months between when there are no events? Anything you desperately want that can make you depressed when you cannot have it has power over you to make you miserable. As good as happiness is, we need something more; it is contentment.

What is contentment? Vocabulary.com/Dictionary explains that contentment is more about "peaceful ease of mind" than "an excited kind of happy." Contentment is about living a satisfying life.

A content person rarely gets bored because his enjoyment comes from his relationships with God and family. This person lives with a purpose; therefore, whatever he does comes from his heart. A content person does an excellent job because he puts his heart into his work. His warm personality toward his loved ones, friends, and people, in general, is evidence that he is at peace with God and himself. On the other hand, happiness is materialistic and self-centered as it depends on the next occasion or event and what people can do for him.

The apostle Paul had experienced abundance and lack, comfort, and discomfort, yet he had learned to be content. Philippians 4:11:12 "...I have learned in whatever state I am, to be content: I know how to be abased, and I know how to abound. Everywhere and in all things I have learned both to be full and to be hungry, both to abound and to suffer need." Contentment does not come naturally, but we learn it in the midst of the trying situation by the grace of God. For example, when Belle and her family were praying for her father's salvation, it did not happen immediately. While waiting, they were developing the fruit of the Spirit qualities, like love, joy, peace, longsuffering or patience, kindness, goodness, faithfulness, gentleness, and self-control. (Galatians 5:22-23). You do not have to like your present situation, but you can be peaceful and satisfied while waiting for change. A person needs to be content with his present situation if he wants to move forward. He can desire a better life and set goals to achieve it, but working toward the goals takes time. Joy, an aspect of the fruit of the spirit, is contentment, which goes beyond happiness as it comes from faith in God during trials. Joy gives you strength during the "working toward" period until you accomplish your goals.

Contentment is a conscious effort one makes each day while dealing with challenges and setbacks. Conscious effort means that the individual has not accepted the unpleasant situation as his final lot in life. He would do whatever is necessary to change the situation, but there is a waiting period before he gets results. During this time, he develops patience, another aspect of the fruit of the Spirit.

Waiting for a breakthrough can be frustrating, so the idea of giving up is tempting. Belle, mentioned in chapter 1, felt helpless in a dysfunctional situation in her home. She kept on praying for God to intervene, but it felt as if He was not answering the prayers of her family. There was a time when she wanted to forget about God, salvation, and her family. Nevertheless, she did not act on her feelings.

She continued with her mother and sisters with prayer. During family devotion, she read interesting scriptures about persistence and endurance, so she began to practice waiting patiently.

Changes began to happen, first in her attitude toward her father. She was resentful toward him for putting his family in a difficult position. Gradually, she began to replace resentment with compassion. Second, Belle's anxiety about her family's unstable situation began to diminish. She recognized that being anxious added to the frustration. By that time, her father had given his life to the Lord, and he had stopped drinking alcohol. His personality was getting better than before.

When Belle and her siblings were children, their father Ralph would take them, along with their mother, to the beach and the countryside occasionally. At other times, he would take them to the savannah to ride their bicycles and fly kites. Frances would take her children to birthday parties and church bazaars. These occasions made them happy, but they would go back to normal life when Ralph would get drunk, and in rage, he would throw household items and food outside of the house. He would also hurl hurtful words at his wife and children. At those difficult times, Frances and her daughters learned contentment by (1) Thanking God for the answer to their prayers, even before the manifestation. (2) They learned to trust God to work out everything for the best. (3) They became satisfied in their present circumstances while waiting for the answer to their prayers. (4) They relied on God to give them the ability to handle adversities well. (5) They helped other distressed people.

(1) First Thessalonians 5:18 reads, "In everything give thanks; for this is the will of God in Christ Jesus for you." Frances and her daughters were thankful to God for His deliverance from Ralph's unpredictable behavior. They were thankful during the difficult time while waiting for the manifestation of the breakthrough. Being thankful during difficult times does two things for us. First, it takes away the anxiety of waiting for answers to prayer, and it helps build up your faith. Second, being thankful builds an optimistic attitude toward life. Optimism keeps you contented. Whatever you practice continuously will become your lifestyle.

You can thank God for countless things, like His protection from things you did not know. Even in disappointments, a person can be thankful. For example, when Belle was nineteen years old, she got the opportunity to go to a concert for the first time. She was so excited about getting her new purple and cream dress. Then she went to the hairdresser for her first haircut so she would look like a young woman and not a girl. Belle bought her ticket one month earlier.

On the day of the concert, one of the cars could not start, and there was no room in any of the other cars for Belle and one other person. She was very disappointed and heartbroken. The next morning Belle heard of an accident that took place on the highway the night before. Most of the vehicles were on their way to the concert. Her friends' cars were involved in the accident. No one was seriously hurt, but it interrupted their plans as the medics took them to the hospital for a check-up and they were unable to go to the concert. Belle was thankful that God protected her from an unpleasant experience. Disappointment never upset Belle again. She learned from that experience that disappointment is one of God's ways of protecting us from danger.

(2) Romans 8:28 reads, "And we know that all things work together for good to those who love God, to those who are the called according to His purpose." Circumstances are a part of life, and sometimes, they are unfavorable. When you have faith in God, He turns the situation around in your favor at the right time.

When Becky was twenty-eight years old, she understood the true meaning of the above scripture. Becky did not have many friends in school and had only one true friend, named Sally. After they finished high school, Becky and Sally lost touch with each other as they went on separate ways. Becky always wanted at least one good friend, who would accompany her to the malls and to travel. To some people, having a friend may be insignificant, but to Becky, it was very important. She was a quiet person who did not interact much. She prefers one or two close friends, which is not a defect; it is just that we all have different personalities due to our genetic makeup, our environment, and the composition of chemicals in our brains. Becky would pray to God to send someone to befriend her, who would be genuine. She prayed that same scripture back to God, asking Him to "work all things for her good."

One day, after Becky's visit to her grandmother, she stopped at an ice-cream shop. A few minutes later, a young woman came up to her and asked, "Are you, Becky?" Becky looked up at her and recognized it was Sally. They were very happy to meet each other again after ten years. Their friendship continued for a long time, and they have visited many places together.

(3) Philippians 4:11-12 reads, "...I have learned in whatever state I am, to be content: I know how to be abased, and I know how to abound. Everywhere and in all things I have learned both to be full and to be hungry, both to abound and to suffer need." It is natural to become upset when things are not going well, therefore, practice being satisfied where you presently are, knowing that the situation will change. Even when the temptation to complain or get frustrated rises up, resist it by changing your mind by doing something you enjoy.

An example is with Danella. Whenever there was an event, like Christmas, a birthday, or a wedding, etc. she was very happy and the life of the occasion, but when they were over, she would get sad of her father's drinking and bad behavior. Later on, Gerard, her brother, developed his father's aggression. Danella would go into depression because of the volatile situation in her family.

One day Danella while she was reading the above scripture, she wanted to know what it meant, so she asked me to help her research what the apostle Paul meant by "I have learned in whatever state I am, to be content." Danella learned that the apostle Paul knew the good life when he was a Pharisee. He was highly educated in the laws of the Pharisees and from the tribe of Benjamin, which meant that he was from a respected and well-off family, and he did not lack anything (Philippians 3:4-6). Later on, as an apostle, Paul experienced many adversities, which included shipwrecks, beatings, physical attacks, and sleepless nights. (Second Corinthians 11:24-27). The apostle Paul learned from His experiences to rely on the Lord to take him through his difficulties.

Even though he faced severe challenges, he became content.

Learning this about the apostle Paul's experiences got Danella's attention. She thought, "I may never experience anything as severe as Paul, yet he became content in his adversities. I can also be at peace in my situation while I am waiting for my breakthrough." She changed her focus from the problems to listening to music, which she enjoyed a lot. Danella overcame depression by finding joy in the Lord.

(4) Philippians 4:13 "I can do all things through Christ who strengthens me." Jesus Christ will give you the strength to handle any difficulty with wisdom and success, but you must believe that He would. Frances learned about believing the above scripture and declaring it; for example, she had a full-time job, four children at school, and an unemployed husband, who demanded cigarettes every week.

Sun or rain, Frances had to go to work to provide for her family. There were school books and uniforms for the children. Rent to pay, then later on a mortgage. She used public transport, which was unreliable at times, to and from work. Frances left her home at six o'clock on mornings and returned at six o'clock on evenings, on the good days. When she got home, she helped her children with their homework and at the same time listened to her complaining husband. When he was not at home, she became concerned, because it meant that he was out drinking.

Ralph would return home late at night in a drunken state, only to wake up his family to criticize and find fault with them. He would threaten Frances that if she left him, he would kidnap her children and she would never see them again. The thought of that was terrifying. If he were in a rage, he would throw household items, including food outside, shouting, "Nobody cares about me!" This commotion would happen late at night, and this was a very stressful time for Frances and her children.

She prayed like this, "Heavenly Father, I thank You that I can keep my sanity and peace of mind through Jesus Christ who strengthens me." She did it successfully. God gave her the ability to rise above the troublesome situation. Frances also prayed for their deliverance and breakthrough, which came eventually. If you ask Frances today, how she managed to deal with that difficult situation, she would say, "I do not know because Jesus Christ gave me the strength to cope with the situation at the time. It is as if I was in auto mode."

(5) Luke 6:38 reads, "Give, and it will be given to you: good measure, pressed down, shaken together, and running over will be put into your bosom. For with the same measure that you use, it will be measured back to you." Frances, Ralph, and their daughters have always been a caring and giving family. They gave of themselves by helping people who were in distress while they were also hurting. They got jobs for different young people; bought stoves and mattresses for two low-income families. They also paid rent for two other families for two and three years each and bought groceries for others. They even contributed to the payment of the debts of others. This financial assistance was some of the material help they extended toward those in need.

Ralph had given his life to the Lord, and while they were praying for Gerard's deliverance from resentment, his family encouraged many persons who were discouraged and depressed. They gave practical support, even when there was turmoil in their home and praying for help.

Contentment or joy is the quality one develops during the transition period between dealing with the present challenges and waiting for circumstances to change for the better. Contentment keeps you strong so you can focus clearly on coping with life's anxieties and it gives you the energy not to give up. (Nehemiah 8:10) The best thing about contentment is that once you developed it, it would remain with you.

CHAPTER 4

HEALING AND DELIVERANCE

THERE IS HOPE FOR HURTING people because God has provided a way to root out condemnation and replace it with freedom from heartache and sorrow to peace and joy in our lives. Self-condemnation is the result of sin and therefore, it is responsible for the negative feelings people have toward themselves. Romans 8:1-3 explains the effects of Jesus Christ death and resurrection on humankind.

Verse 1, "There is therefore now no condemnation to those who are in Christ Jesus, who do not walk according to the flesh, but according to the Spirit." It is necessary to understand the meaning of the term "in Christ Jesus" for you to live free from condemnation. Galatians 3:26-27 give us some insight, "In Christ Jesus, you are all children of God through faith, for all of you who were baptized into Christ have clothed yourselves with Christ." When we have faith in Jesus Christ, we receive His identity, which is the same as "clothed yourself with Christ." Our new identity will cause us to overcome condemnation.

Verse 2, "For the law of the Spirit of life in Christ Jesus has made me free from the law of sin and death." We cannot get rid of self-condemnation with human ability. "The Spirit of life in Christ Jesus" is resurrection life, the same life in Jesus

Christ, which raised Him from the dead. We receive this life through the Holy Spirit when we give ourselves to Him, which breaks and destroys sin and condemnation. He took our condemnation upon Himself and pardoned us from a prison of gloom and hopelessness.

Verse 3, "For what the law could not do in that it was weak through the flesh, God did by sending His own Son in the likeness of sinful flesh, on account of sin: He condemned sin in the flesh," Human weaknesses cannot deliver anyone from his shortcomings. However, Jesus Christ condemned sin in His human body to give us the deliverance from sin and condemnation. A saved person can now overcome bad traits and addictions with the new life he received from Christ Jesus. Now, this is good news.

As you understand Romans 8:1-3, you are ready to move forward in life. You need to know two things for you to be successful. The first one is that God loves you unconditionally. If He did not love you, Jesus Christ would not have left the infinity of heaven to become a human and experience a humiliating and painful death for us. Romans 5:6, 8-9 "For when we were still without strength, in due time Christ died for the ungodly. But God demonstrates

His own love toward us, in that while we were still sinners, Christ died for us. Much more then, having now been justified by His blood, we shall be saved from wrath through Him." The beginning of Christ's suffering until His death began in the Garden of Gethsemane, His arrest, then the insults, scourging and finally when the soldiers nailed Him to the cross, and He died. (Matthew 26:36-39; 67; 27:26-50; Mark 14:16-30; Luke 22:63-65; 23:10-11; 44-46). Jesus' action to subject Himself to a disgraceful and painful ordeal is the expression of His love for us. You may wonder, "Why did Jesus have to suffer?" He suffered because sin causes humankind to suffer. Jesus Christ took sin upon Himself on our behalf. While on the cross dying, Jesus said: "It is finished!" And bowing His head, He gave up His spirit." "It is finished!" means that He was successful in paying for all of our sins and the effect of our sins. Condemnation is the root effect of sin.

After three days, the Holy Spirit raised Jesus Christ from the dead, which is a guarantee that He paid for all of our sins with His life, and God was satisfied with the payment, which is additional evidence of God's love for us. (John 3:16). God's love toward us justified or made us righteous by the blood of Jesus Christ. Romans 8:32-39 also shows us how much

God loves us. The Apostle Paul's experiences had convinced him that there is nothing in the world to interrupt God's love for us. Verses 38-39 "For I am persuaded that neither death nor life, nor angels nor principalities nor powers, nor things present nor things to come, nor height nor depth, nor any other created thing, shall be able to separate us from the love of God which is in Christ Jesus our Lord."

Some people wonder, what does sin have to do with our problems? Sin has everything to do with it, and it is the cause of self-condemnation, which in turn creates all the troubles in life. Sin is both a verb and a noun. The verb sin is the bad thing that a person does, like cheating, stealing, deception, malicious, etc. The noun sin is who the person is, an inherent part of every one of us, which we received from Adam and Eve. When John the Baptist saw Jesus approaching Him for baptism, he said, "Behold! The Lamb of God who takes away the sin of the world!" (John 1:29) "Sin" in John 1:29 is the noun. God made provision through Jesus Christ's death to root out sin, the noun, from off our lives and made us righteous through Jesus Christ. Righteousness becomes our identity instead of sin. Romans 5:8 continue to say, "While we were still sinners Christ died for us." God did not expect us to clean up our lives before we accept Jesus because He knew that we could not help ourselves. If we could have done it, Jesus would not have had to come as a man to die for us, but it was while we were in bondage to sin and all the problems that go along with it, that Jesus came to free us from its hold. (John 8:36). Jesus' death was the expression of God's love toward us. First John 4:19 "We love Him because He first loved us." When you understand the extent of God's love for you and you accept it, you will love Him, and then you will love yourself.

Loving yourself is not a pompous and stuck up attitude where you feel you are better than others are and look down on them. No, it is recognizing and accepting your value to God. If it were not for Jesus Christ paying the price for your sin, you would be stuck forever in despair. When you love yourself, you will develop self-worth, which replaces self-condemnation. The basis for our self-worth is not on external conditions; like people's opinion of us or our social status, material possessions, and physical appearance. It is not about what we think about ourselves; it is about God's love for us. Evidence of someone who lacks self-worth is the unworthy way he sees himself. In his mind, he thinks he is ugly and stupid. Therefore, he cannot accept sincere compliments because he thinks he does not deserve any. Jesus said, "Are not five sparrows sold for two copper coins? And not one of them is forgotten before God. But the very hairs of your head are all numbered. Do not fear therefore; you are of more value than many sparrows." (Luke 12:6-7) Back then, the Israelites were still under the Mosaic Law, and a sacrifice for one's sin was necessary. Sparrows were very cheap, and they had little value, and the poor people could afford to buy for their sacrifices. God cares for His creation so much that He noticed even this little bird, yet Jesus did not die for any other creature, but humans. Humans are God's greatest work in creation, and He values us so much more; therefore, He saw us worthy of His Son's sacrifice on our behalf. God even knows the exact amount of strands of hair, which are on our heads, which speaks of intimacy. We do not even know because our hair drops and grows back, so the number changes every day. God is interested in every detail of our lives, regardless of how insignificant it may seem. Accept God's love in your life and receive your healing and deliverance.

To understand what Jesus' sufferings involve and how we benefit from it, we will read the prophecy from Isaiah 53:4-5 "Surely He has borne our griefs and carried our sorrows; yet we esteemed Him stricken, smitten by God, and afflicted. But He was wounded for our transgressions; He was bruised for our iniquities; the chastisement of our peace was upon Him, and by His stripes, we are healed."

Verse Four. The original Hebrew word for "griefs" means "malady, anxiety, calamity...." This verse shows us that Jesus carried for us all the sicknesses, anxieties and distress we face. Matthew 8:17 shows that while Jesus was on earth, He healed many sick and demon-possessed people. "Stricken," "smitten," and "afflicted" mean that when the Roman officers arrested Jesus, people saw this as God was punishing Him. In reality, Jesus was sinless, so He did not suffer and died for Himself, but He did it for us. Jesus represented humanity, so He willingly offered Himself for the world. (Read John 6:38).

Verse Five. Chapter 4. When the soldiers spat on Jesus and pulled at His beard at Mark 15:19-20, it was the fulfillment of Isaiah 53:5. "Transgression" means "to break the law," so Jesus took our punishment because as sinners, we broke God's law. Jesus Christ experienced suffering from the time of His arrest in the Garden of Gethsemane. He went before the Sanhedrin to Pilate to Herod and back to Pilate again to interrogate Him before they scourged and then crucified Him (Luke 22:66-71; Luke 23).

"Chastisement" means correction, which represents punishment. Jesus did nothing to deserve punishment, but He took the punishment for humans. "Stripes" means weal or beat until black and blue marks remain on the body. The Roman soldiers beat Jesus black and blue until His flesh, tendons, ligaments and blood vessels ripped to shreds. Most prisoners died during the scourging. This brutal beating which Jesus took was for our healing – physical, mental, and emotional. The suffering of Jesus Christ was ugly because the effects of sin are ugly. As we see in this scripture, the crucifixion is that Jesus Christ took upon Himself all that we deserved, our punishment, and gave us all that He deserves – His righteousness. Romans 3:22 "for all have sinned and fall short of the glory of God.' When Jesus lived on earth, He called God, His Father. However, when He was on the cross taking all our punishment, He cried out, "My God, My God, why have You forsaken me?" (Matthew 27:46) On the cross, was the only time Jesus called His Father, "God," because God is holy and He cannot be in the presence of sin. At that moment, Jesus was carrying our sin; so God could not be around His beloved Son, and it was heartbreaking for Jesus.

Jesus knows that we live in a physical world and have material needs and wants. That is why everything Jesus Christ did for us was an exchange. He sweated blood in the Garden of Gethsemane to break the curse from Adam after he sinned. God told Adam in Genesis 3:19 that "In the sweat of your face you shall eat bread till you return to the ground..." (Luke 22:44) Jesus received a crown of thorns on his head to break the curse of mental anguish and stress from off our lives. (Genesis 3:18; Matthew 27:29) When the Roman soldiers beat Jesus to shreds, it was to replace our sicknesses with good health. Genesis 2:17; Isaiah 53:5; John 19:1) God told Adam that in the day he eats of the tree of knowledge of good and evil he "shall surely die." Sickness leads to death, so Jesus died as a young man so we can have a long and satisfying life. (Psalm 91:16). Therefore, Jesus' brutal death for us is God's incomparable love toward us. Jesus replaced self-condemnation with love and self-worth.

Frances used to have low self-worth and was timid. She was afraid to offend anyone at the expense of her comfort and peace of mind. When she accepted God's love toward her, she began to love herself. She thought to herself, "Jesus Christ loves me so much that he deemed me worthy of taking away my distresses and limitations to give me a meaningful life. He became a human so that He could identify with my weaknesses. Now, he has replaced my shortcomings with His strength. I deserve all God's best." From then on, Frances gradually grew from being timid and having low self-worth to one with confidence and high self-worth. Now, Frances is not afraid of offending anyone. She realizes that it is unrealistic to please every person we meet. Therefore, some people may feel hurt.

For instance, one young woman, the mother of a three-year-old daughter, and a single parent is a spendthrift. She is a low-income worker, who would not make a budget. She pays her rent, but has little money for groceries, as she spends her money on non-essential items. Frances advises the young woman how to make a budget to suit her income, but she ignores her. The young woman borrows money regularly and is always in debt. The woman goes to Frances to borrow money to pay off her debts, and Frances said, "No." Frances is not harsh because she helped her in the past, but for the woman to learn to manage her money well, she would not support her in her bad habit. A spendthrift is equal to an addiction like being an alcoholic or a gambler. Frances felt that giving the woman money to spend carelessly is like buying vodka for an alcoholic. The cycle of borrowing and paying back will be continuous if you do not put a stop to it.

Frances understood struggle well. She took care of four children and an unemployed husband for years. She learned to manage her money well, as she made her mortgage payments, paid her utility bills, bought groceries, and educate her children, etc. There were times when she needed to borrow money, which she paid back. Frances explained to her children about knowing their priorities. When Frances got bonuses, she would treat her family to nice things. Thank God, her financial situation improved. Frances talks to young women about managing their lives and knowing their priorities. Those who take her advice, move forward successfully.

The second thing you need to know so you can move forward successfully is the need to forgive those who hurt you. Forgiveness is necessary for your healing, but before you can forgive those who hurt you, you need to receive God's forgiveness of your sins through the blood of Jesus Christ. You can only give what we have but cannot give what we do not have. For example, if I have a lime tree, you can get limes, but if you want oranges, I cannot give them to you, because I do not have an orange tree. When we first receive God's forgiveness, it will equip us to forgive ourselves for all the mistakes and wrong decisions we have made, and we will be able to forgive those who have hurt us. Unforgiveness, bitterness, and resentment add to your hurt while the one who caused the injury has forgotten you and moved on in life. Even if that person suffers and pays for the bad he did to you, it will not change the damage done to you from the hurt, so it is better for you to forgive him and let God bring healing and restoration to your life. Forgiveness is a choice, so use it to set yourself free from your hurts. God will deal with the wrongdoer because of Romans 12:19 reads, "Vengeance is Mine, I will repay," says the Lord."

Faith in God's Word, the Bible gives us access to God's forgiveness through Jesus Christ. Hebrews 11:1 reads, "Now faith is the substance of things hoped for, the evidence of things not seen." The phrase stated in this scripture verse, "substance of things hoped for" are the promises of God in the Bible. In regards to receiving forgiveness, we should have the confident assurance that God has already forgiven us based on the death of His beloved Son. John 3:16-17 "For God so loved the world that He gave His only begotten Son, that whoever believes in Him should not perish but have everlasting life.

For God did not send His Son into the world to condemn the world, but that the world through Him might be saved." When we know that God has forgiven us of our sins, then we can easily forgive others. Colossians 3:13 "...even as Christ forgave you, so you also must do."

Many people think forgiveness means that the offender has gotten away with his wicked act toward you, but this is not so. You are the one who benefits because you are set free from the pain, which consumes a person. Resentment, bitterness, and hatred are the results of unforgiveness. Anybody can see it on his or her facial expression, like a frown or scowl, and negative body language. Whenever he hears the person's name and sees him, he feels animosity toward him. When someone thinks and repeatedly talks about the injustice or the unfair treatment which he received, is evidence of unforgiveness. This person hurts only himself, and it manifests in physical, mental, and emotional sicknesses. On the other hand, forgiveness is to release the individual from your heart for your freedom from a prison of sadness and misery. When it is hard to forgive someone, you should ask God to give you a forgiving heart. For example, "Thank You, Father, for forgiving me for all my sins through the blood of Jesus Christ. Thank You for healing me from my childhood hurts and the unfair treatment I got from others. I cannot do anything about what has happened in the past, but You can. I offer up my life to You. Your word said that I should forgive others for their shortcomings just as Christ has forgiven me. I do not know how to forgive anyone because I am very angry and hurt, but please help me and give me the willingness and the ability to forgive. Thank You in the name of Jesus Christ. Amen." When you pray with humility and honesty, be sure that God will answer your prayer request and it will be easier for you to forgive.

Nevertheless, depending on who the wrongdoer is, you do not have to embrace the person and be his or her friend. Forgiveness does not change the one who hurt you, as he may still be harmful and can be a danger to you so that you will avoid any contact with that person. If the offender is violent, a rapist or a murderer, common sense will tell you that you should keep far away from him; however, you do not harbor any hatred toward him when you forgive him. Whenever you forgive an offender, you free yourself from mental torment. You benefit by forgiving your enemies and moving on with your life, then trust God to work things out for your good. When you forgive, your deliverance will manifest.

Even though people hurt us, the devil is the instigator. He works behind the scenes through people and circumstances. Second Corinthians 10:3-4 reads, "For though we walk in the flesh, we do not war according to the flesh. For the weapons of our warfare are not carnal but mighty in God for pulling down strongholds." This scripture means that even though our lives are physical, we are in a spiritual war. The devil is relentlessly attacking us because we are a threat to him. He is afraid that if he leaves us alone, we will overcome the obstacles he put in our path, and we would gain strength and cause damage to the kingdom of darkness. God equips us to ward off the attacks of the devil. He gave us a spiritual armor to protect ourselves from the invisible enemy. Remember, God is more powerful than the devil and whatever he throws at us would fail. Isaiah 54:17 "No weapon formed against you shall prosper, and every tongue which rises against you in judgment you shall condemn. This is the heritage of the servants of the LORD, and their righteousness is from Me," says the LORD." For instance, when Belle understood this verse, she realized that "weapons" and "tongues" did form against her family, but according to the scripture, they will not prosper. She prayed the scripture by saying, "Heavenly Father, You said that no weapon formed against me should prosper. The addiction and verbal abuse in my family are weapons and lying words formed against us. I declare that they would fail and be ineffective because I am the righteousness of God in Christ Jesus in the name of Jesus Christ." Later on, malicious "tongues" rose up against her family, and she prayed the same way, and the negative words did not prosper but failed. Belle was persistent in her prayer and Bible reading, and she saw good results each time.

The scripture at Ephesians 6:10-18 states seven parts of the full armor of God to protect us from the devil. The apostle Paul used an illustration of the ancient Roman soldiers. They are (1) to "gird your waist with truth." Jesus said the Word of God or the Bible is the truth. The truth in the Bible holds up the rest of the armor just as a belt would hold up a pair of trousers. (John 17:17) Since the Word of God is the truth, then we need to know the scripture by reading and meditating regularly. (2) "Put on the breastplate of righteousness." Second Corinthians 5:21 says that we are the righteousness of God in Christ Jesus. We are not righteous with our good works but the righteousness we received from believing in the death and resurrection of Jesus Christ. The breastplate protects your physical heart, so righteousness protects your spiritual heart. (3) "Shod your feet with the preparation of the gospel of peace." We walk with our feet. "Walk" represents our daily activities, which means that we should always be prepared to share the Word of God with those we meet. We do not preach down to people, because they may find it annoying and they will avoid us, but in everyday interaction with others, we can share a scripture or Bible principle in context with the conversation. (4) "The shield of faith with which you will be able to quench all the fiery darts of the wicked one." Hebrews 11:6 tells us "Without faith, it is impossible to please God..." Faith in God's Word is a shield to protect us. "The fiery darts" are the attacks from the devil that come against us in various ways, through people or circumstances. Our faith in God will prevent "the fiery darts" from hurting us. For instance, you see a potential car accident and immediately the scripture from Psalm 91:11 comes to your mind, "For He shall give His angels charge over you, to keep you in all your ways." The accident did not happen because, in the unseen world, the angels protect you by preventing the accident. (5) "Take the helmet of salvation." Salvation protects your mind because the devil tries filling it with fear, doubt, and negative thoughts. You receive salvation by believing in Jesus Christ then His promises to you fill your minds with faith and hope (Jeremiah 29:11). (6) "The sword of the Spirit, which is the word of God." Unlike the other parts of the full armor of God, which protects us, the sword attacks the enemy. We attack the devil by quoting scripture. For example, if you get a symptom of a sore throat, the first thing that comes to mind is, "I am catching a cold." You remember Isaiah 53:5 "By the stripes of Jesus Christ I am healed." Declare it, then give God thanks for your healing, and sometime during the day, the sore throat will clear up. (7) "Praying always with all prayer and supplication in the Spirit." You cannot pray every single moment of the day because you have other things to do. This text means you need to have a prayerful attitude during the day. You can pray while going to work or school, and ask God for guidance before you begin to work so you would do an effective job. You can also pray and sing praise and worship songs while doing your chores at home or running errands.

The Bible refers the devil as "the god of this age" and "the prince of the power of the air" (Second Corinthians 4:4 and Ephesians 2:2). We find the weapons God gave us to fight this invisible battle are in the Bible. They are (1) The Holy Bible, (2) Prayer, (3) Church attendance, and (4) Our words. The following is an explanation of how these four weapons work.

(1) The Holy Bible: Another word for The Bible is the Word of God. (Colossians 4:3; 1 Thessalonians 2:13) The Bible is more than rules, regulations and good stories, which are written, in a holy book. There is absolute power in the Word of God. First Thessalonians 1:5 "For our gospel did not come to you in word only, but also in power, and in the Holy Spirit and much assurance…" "Power" is the essential attribute in the Word of God. To benefit from that power, you need to know what is on the pages of the Bible. There is no power if your Bible is on display on your bookshelf. You need to get the written words into your mind and heart. When the scripture is in your heart, then it becomes powerful. How do I get the scripture from the pages of the Bible into my heart? Read, meditate and study the Bible. The Holy Spirit will bring to your memory the particular verse of scripture for any situation you are in at that moment. Reading, meditating, and studying the scripture is like eating food to nourish your body. Jesus said in Luke 4:4 "It is written, 'Man shall not live by bread alone, but by every word of God." When you read and meditate on the Bible, it will enter into your heart, and you will not forget it. The

Holy Spirit will remind you of the scripture for the specific situation.

For example, one of Belle's cousins, a young woman, named Kristina, with first class honors in business from the university she attended, had a job interview with a prestigious company with a high salary. When she got to her appointment, she met fifteen other persons in the waiting room for the same position. She got a little nervous and silently prayed, "My God, help me please." She immediately remembered Psalm 56:3 "Whenever I am afraid, I will trust in You." Then she suddenly became calm without making any effort. One or two things could have happened in this situation; she could have gotten the job or even if she did not get it, God would provide her with a better job. In Kristina's case, she got the job. The way she handled this matter is spiritual warfare against nervousness.

Most people know what it means to read and study, but not many know the meaning of meditating on the Bible. "Meditate" means to "think carefully about." You read a scripture passage and think carefully about it. When we read and meditate on the Bible regularly, it strengths us spiritually so we will be able to handle life successfully as a whole. In the example mentioned above, Psalm 56:3 came to Kristina's mind immediately because she read and meditated on the Word of God in her private time.

(2) Prayer: Trials and tribulation come in many forms, and prayer is a weapon we can use to fight. Philippians 4:6-7 " Be anxious for nothing, but in everything by prayer and supplication, with thanksgiving, let your requests be made known to God and the peace of God, which surpasses all understanding, will guard your hearts and minds through Christ Jesus." Worry is another word for anxious. The first thing that happens in any trial is to panic and worry, but God wants us to pray. We ask God for help in a humble manner. "With thanksgiving" means that we should be thankful for the answer to our prayers while we are waiting to receive the answer. "Waiting" means that we should go about our everyday affairs with a good attitude of calm expectation until the answer to our prayers becomes a reality. Thanksgiving is a

very important part of praying because we focus on God rather than the problem.

Thanksgiving strengthens our faith. Belle prayed like this when she used to pray for her brother, Gerard's salvation. He was angry and resentful toward his father and with God. Her prayer request would be something like this, "I thank You Father that it is your will for Gerard to give his life to You because Your word said that God is "not willing that any should perish but that all should come to repentance." (Second Peter 3:9) Please draw Gerard by Your Holy Spirit, and deliver him from resentment and anger and give him a forgiving heart, in the name of Jesus Christ. Amen." The answer to some prayers takes time because God will not override a person's free will. The person must make that decision based on the promptings of the Holy Spirit in his heart. In the meantime, she would give God thanks for the answer. "Heavenly Father, I thank You for the precious blood of Jesus. Thank You for salvation. Thank You for drawing Gerard toward Jesus. (John 6:44) Thank You for fulfilling Your promises, as the scripture said Your word should prosper in the thing for which You sent it, in the

name of Jesus. Amen." (Isaiah 55:10-11)."
Sometimes you might wait for days, weeks,
months and even years before you get an
answer to your prayers. The reason for
waiting has two purposes. The first reason
is to develop virtues in you, like patience
and humility or compassion and kindness
toward others and faith in God. The second
reason for waiting for the answer to your
prayers is that God is prompting the other
person involved, and He is waiting for him
to respond. After about two years of praying,
Gerard gave his life to Jesus Christ.

Praise and worship of God are an essential
part of prayer. There are many accounts in the
Bible of battles won by praise and worship to
God. One account was at Second Chronicles
20 when enemy nations conspired to fight
with King Jehoshaphat of Judah. Jehoshaphat
knew that his enemies outnumbered him and
his troops, and they did not have a chance,
and he panicked. He did the best thing by
outpouring his heart to God in prayer. All
of Judah got ready for battle with God's
direction to put the worship singers to lead
the gathering to sing praises to God. While
Jehoshaphat and his people sang unto the

Lord, the enemy nations turned against and killed each other and Judah got the victory.

The Bible contains many references to singing. Psalm 96:1-2 "Oh, sing to the LORD a new song! Sing to the LORD, all the earth. Sing to the LORD, bless His name; proclaim the good news of His salvation from day-to-day." The New Testament commands us to sing psalms, hymns, and spiritual songs at Ephesians 5:19 and Colossians 3:16. Praise and worship are scripture in song. It is easy to sing when all is well, but when we are in distress, and we sing to the Lord, we do spiritual warfare and confuse the enemy (the devil and his demons behind the problems we face). Just as how Jehoshaphat got the victory, we will also get the victory and overcome our challenges.

After we pray and give thanks to God, notice, "the peace of God which surpasses all understanding will guard your heart and mind through Christ Jesus." The scripture did not just say "peace," but the "peace of God." The peace of God will give you rest and calmness because it is supernatural, which Jesus Christ alone can give. Isaiah

9:6 said that His name is "...the Prince of Peace." The peace of God is not the absence of problems or turmoil, but it is peace in the midst of the situation, which is a powerful position to be. Be persistent in prayer and thanksgiving and the bad situation would turn around at the right time.

Jesus said, "These things I have spoken to you, that in Me you may have peace. In the world, you will have tribulation, but be of good cheer, I have overcome the world." (John 16:33) The original Greek word for "world" means "orderly arrangement." The world, in John 16:33, is not the planet earth, but the orderly arrangement of how things operate on the earth. The world cannot even imagine the peace Jesus Christ gives because it says to worry when problems arise, but the Bible says do not be anxious about anything. The world says that the country is in a recession, prepare for hard times, but the Bible says, "my God will supply all your need according to His riches in glory by Christ Jesus." (Philippians 4:19) About the various strains of viruses, the world becomes fearful, but the Bible says, He (the Lord) delivers me from the perilous pestilence or deadly sicknesses. (Psalm 91:3) One has to give his life to Jesus Christ to experience the peace of God. Jesus promise of peace guards your heart and mind against worry. Worry blocks faith because faith in God will bring the answer to your prayers. "Surpasses all understanding," means that even though you have not seen any sign of change in the situation yet, your faith in God gives you the confidence that He will answer your prayers at the right time. The devil knows that he has lost when he cannot disturb your peace. Do not worry.

Belle experienced the peace of God during the trying times, which her family experienced. Belle would declare the appropriate scripture for her father's deliverance from addiction and his bad attitude toward his family. In the midst of the situation, she received the peace of God in her heart, since she was persistent in prayer with thanksgiving. Even though her father was still behaving the same way, she had faith in God that her family would get their breakthrough. At that same time, people were speaking negatively about Ralph. They were saying words like, "He will never change," "He is bad since he was a child,"

"He is wicked, and he would go to hell," etc. Even though she felt bad, she never gave up on trusting God. The victory came through, and she saw her father got his deliverance from his inadequacies. Belle's persistence in prayer during a seemingly hopeless situation is spiritual warfare.

(3) Church attendance: Acts 2:47 "...And the Lord added to the church daily those who were being saved." The church is God's idea and not man's. The Lord is the one who saves and adds to the congregation. Even though some leaders of the church portray a poor example of Christianity, they are in the minority. The world thrives on bad news, so they bring to light the few bad examples, but they leave out the good, which is the majority. Many people in the world are not interested in the many amazing things God is doing through the church.

Jesus said in Matthew 18:20 "For where two or three are gathered together in My name, I am there in the midst of them." The building is where saved people congregate to praise and worship God and to learn from the scripture. Therefore, the people are the church. Jesus Christ gave grace gifts to all Christians for the benefit of the church. Grace gifts mean that God gives them freely to His church. We do not work for them, and we did not earn them. The Bible calls them the gifts of the Spirit. The offices of pastors and reverends are gifts from God to preach and teach by explaining the Bible to their congregation. These are the pulpit gifts. There are also other gifts of the Spirit listed in the scripture in the parenthesis which can operate in all Christians (Ephesians 4:7-15, Romans 12:3-8 and 1 Corinthians 12:4-11). Healing and miracles are two of the gifts of the Spirit. In the church, we cast out demonic forces, which lock people into oppression and depression, in the name of Jesus Christ. They are the evil spirits responsible for all your problems. Church attendance is a part of spiritual warfare.

(4) Our words – Proverbs 18:21 "Death and life are in the power of the tongue and those who love it will eat its fruit." What we speak will affect our lives, so we should pay attention to what we say. We will become whatever we say about ourselves. Listen to how people speak in general, "I am suffering

from asthma," "I am dying to eat some sweet and juicy mangoes," "I cannot believe that I am so stupid," "My salary is so small. I can barely meet my monthly commitments," "I am starving from hunger," etc. Look at these words, "suffering, dying, stupid, small salary, barely, and starving." These words are awful, but we make remarks like this about ourselves all the time. No wonder people are sick, suffering, do not have enough, and are in debt. We are not pretending that these issues do not exist. The more negative words one uses to describe the present situation, the longer he would remain there. That person feels weighed down and tires out frequently by the problems.

When we speak healing and success into our present circumstances, they will change to what we are saying. Change what we say about ourselves. This principle also applies to what we say to our loved ones. Instead, we could say, "By the stripes of Jesus Christ I am healed from asthma," "I am longing to eat some sweet and juicy mangoes," "Jesus Christ is my wisdom," "thank God I can manage my money," "I am very hungry." When we speak this way healing and breakthrough will come, we will make wise decisions, and manage our finances properly.

Our words are powerful because God made us in His image and likeness. (Genesis 1:26-27). Since God used His Word to create the universe and He made us in His image, and then we "create" our life conditions with our words. Read Genesis 1:1-25. Think carefully about what we say. I will give a personal experience about this. One day, I saw two thieves who were on my avocado tree. I threw stones at them and shouted out "Michael! There are thieves in our yard!" There is no "Michael," but I said that to scare them off and it worked. They did not come back. One year later, I needed a tenant for my apartment. After my realtor had screened a few potentials, he approved of a young man named Michael, and he got the apartment. He is a good person. Did you see what happened? "Michael" imaginary became Michael in reality. I spoke him into existence. My word went to work right away from the time I shouted "Michael!" until he arrived at my home. He did not come that same day or even the next week, but a year later. God maneuvered conditions where I needed a tenant. At the same time, He gave Michael the need for an apartment in my neighborhood.

You can start practicing by speaking the things you want instead of saying what you see presently. For example, another of Belle's cousins, a young man, named Anthony, who was shy and did not say much to anyone, except his mother, his sisters, his grandmother and me. Those around ignored him and did not think anything significant about him. One day, about eight years ago, I explained to him about the power of our words, especially when we speak the scripture to ourselves. I highlighted the scripture from Philippians 4:13 "I can do all things through Christ who strengthens me." Anthony began to say to himself, "I can speak boldly to anyone I meet through Christ who strengthens me." "I am brave; I am an encourager; people respect me, etc." Today, people respect Anthony because he is a brave young man in his late-twenties, who encourages many. He now works with his uncle in the family business. He also distributes tracts to young men on the streets in his neighborhood and talks to them about salvation through Jesus Christ.

People now look up to Anthony. One who was insignificant has now become significant. Speaking good words into your life and the life of your loved ones is spiritual warfare.

Ralph, Frances, and their daughters accepted God's love in their lives. They learned about spiritual warfare, and they received their healing and deliverance from their past hurts. They found freedom from resentment and bitterness to joy and peace. Ralph and Frances' family also got their deliverance from timidity and feelings of inadequacy to boldness and competence. When you give your life to Jesus Christ, He will free you from a prison of misery with its bad traits, addictions, negative emotions and dwelling on past disappointments, etc. For instance, Ralph was able to forgive his parents and his siblings. Then they began to show him and his family respect as they saw big changes in his life. The extent of Ralph's change was so obvious that in his old age, women began to look at Ralph, wishing they could get a good husband like him. Frances' was also able to forgive her parents and her husband. Her colleagues and friends admire her for her pleasant personality, along with the insight and wisdom she possesses. Even Delores came to her senses and stopped visiting the soothsayers when she realized that it was futile and she had already wasted too much money. She mellowed down from being strange to being normal to the point that she was able to take good care of her grandchildren. It is better to happen late than it never happened at all.

Belle was able to forgive her father for being verbally abusive toward her family. She got her deliverance from being timid and embarrassed by her father to honoring him before his faultfinders. Belle epitomizes encouragement. She also forgave his siblings for insulting him for too many years to the point that she gave his older sister and three of his older brothers, moral support, and encouragement in their old age. Wherever she goes, people are happy to see her, even if she does not say a word. She speaks with substance, so they feel motivated to move forward, even when they are disheartened. Belle operates in the word of wisdom and the word of knowledge, which are gifts of the Spirit. That means when she meets with anyone; the Holy Spirit gives her the specific words to say to the individual regarding his present situation with the appropriate words of encouragement.

Becky also forgave her father and the children who teased her when she was in school. She finished high school with confidence. She went on to further her studies in career enhancement and micro-entrepreneur. She belonged to a women's group, who stands up for abused women and children.

Becky is also a prayer leader, and she operates in the gift of faith. The gift of faith is a special faith, where God honors the person's word as His own and miraculously brings to pass what he prayed. For example, in a prayer group, which Becky belongs to, they were praying for the members of a local church who lost their jobs due to the recession. When Becky prayed for each one to find another job soon, she did not doubt that God would answer her prayer request. One week later, three persons got jobs and within the next two months, every person Becky prayed for got good jobs.

Danella also forgave her father and her classmates for disregarding her as a child. She got her physical healing from an overactive bladder. She is a pre-school teacher, and both parents and students love her. She has the gift of discerning of spirits, which gives her insight into the source of the problems behind the background of each child. Therefore, she can teach and interact with each child to bring out the best out of him.

Jesus Christ said, "Therefore if the Son makes you free, you shall be free indeed." (John 6:36) There is complete freedom from hurts, sadness, and misery through Jesus Christ.

Sometimes depression could be the symptom of a serious mental condition, so it is wise to visit a doctor. We do not want to be over spiritual that we reject medical treatment completely. There are those who believe that visiting a doctor, is lacking faith in God, but that is not so. Nowhere in the Bible says that Christians should not see a doctor when they are sick. We pray for healing but the waiting may take some time because we are in spiritual warfare against evil spiritual forces. The devil does not want us to overcome our deficiencies so that he would fight relentlessly, and we would be even more persistent in prayer so that we do not give up. Therefore, medication along with professional counseling manages the condition so the individual could function normally until their healing manifests.

C H A P T E R 5

THE LORD IS MY SHEPHERD

WHEN DAVID WAS A BOY, he used to care for his father's sheep. Those days he spent most of his time alone with the sheep, and he used to play the harp, sing and pray. This pastime was how he developed a close relationship with God; and for this reason, he became the most famous king in the world. David wrote seventy-five of the psalms, which were his personal experiences with God in song. Centuries later, New Testament writers quoted many of David's sayings. For example, at Luke 1:49 in Mary's song, she said, "...holy is His name." she quoted David in Psalms 99:3 and 111:9. Also, in Romans 4:6-8, when the apostle Paul explained salvation, that God credits righteousness to the one who accepts Jesus Christ in his life apart from his good works, he quoted David's words at Psalm 32:1,2.

Many years later, King David wrote Psalm Twenty-Three when he was an old man, called, "The Lord is my Shepherd." He was reminiscing about past events where the Lord helped him to kill many "lions, bears, and giants." Second Samuel, chapter 8 records a list of King David's battles, which he won against enemy nations who wanted to conquer Israel. Second Samuel 23:8-39 lists David's mighty men who joined him.

David learned to trust God while tending to his father's sheep as a boy. He likened God to a shepherd who took care of him the same way he took care of his sheep. David had fond memories of how God had miraculously delivered him from his enemies in the past, and he had the confidence that God will also deliver him again. During this time, David developed good qualities, like kindness, thoughtfulness, and fairness, etc. which made him into a likable young man. Just like David, God took care of us in the past, or we would not be here today. Therefore, we have some experience in trusting God to deliver us from difficulties, and He has done so.

Many people today recite "The Lord Is My Shepherd" as a prayer. In this chapter, we will find out what it means for the Lord to be your shepherd and how it helps you to become a better person, by breaking up the verses to get a clearer understanding.

Verse One – "The LORD is my shepherd; I shall not want." The ancient Hebrew language did not have any vowels in their writing. The LORD here in Hebrew is YHWH (the Tetragrammaton, which means four letters). The Jews back then were afraid to misuse the name of God according to one of the commands in the Ten Commandments at Exodus 20:7, so they replaced YHWH with LORD. Got Questions.org, states, "The most likely choice for how the Tetragrammaton was pronounced is "YAH-way," "YAH-weh.""

Today we do not need to call God by His name, Yahweh because Jesus introduced Him to us as our Heavenly Father. Jesus' prayer to God for His disciples at John 17:6 "I have manifested Your name to the men whom You have given Me out of the world." In all of Jesus' prayers, while on earth, He addressed God as Father and not as Yahweh. (Matthew 6:9; Matthew 11:25; Mark 14:36; Luke 23:46; and John 11:41). There is more involved in Jesus manifesting God's name to us than saying His name. Jesus showed us the character of the Person, our heavenly Father, so today when we pray we address God as "Heavenly Father." When Jesus cleansed the leper, healed the sick, delivered those who were demon-possessed, fed the hungry, stopped the storm, and raised the dead, He displayed everything about God's personality. The attributes of God's character is love, mercy, goodness, wisdom, power, and justice, so when David said, "The LORD is my shepherd" he meant that our Heavenly Father, along with His marvelous qualities, was his shepherd.

By introducing God as Father, Jesus made it clear to us that there should be an intimate relationship between God and us just as human parents would have with their children. For example, a child will not call his father or mother by their first names, saying, "Leonard, may I ride my bike?" or "Sharon, may I play in the yard?" Instead, he will say, "Daddy, may I ride my bike?" or "Mommy, may I play in the yard?" Similarly, when we go to our Heavenly Father in prayer, we do not address Him by His name Yahweh, but Father. Mathew 6:9 "Our Father in heaven, hallowed be Your name."

What does it mean by "my shepherd?" The job of a shepherd is to care for his sheep. Caring for the sheep involves feeding the lambs and the sheep. The shepherd also takes them to good pasturelands and water. He grooms and clips them, delivers young ones, leads and teaches them to stay together, goes after the ones who have wandered off, and protects the sheep in the field from predators. Today, Jesus Christ has already died and risen from the dead, so He is our shepherd. At John 10:11 Jesus said, "I am the good shepherd. The good shepherd gives His life for the sheep." Jesus does more for us than a shepherd does for his sheep. He cares for us so much that He gave up His life for us to have a great life because He is "the good shepherd." This great life covers every single area of our lives. One area we can look at is the direction in making important decisions. For instance, when Danella was thinking about her career, she prayed for direction. Her desire to help children led her to early childhood education and child psychology, which turned out to be rewarding as she gets good results. The Good Shepherd, Jesus Christ, directed her steps to become a good teacher, where she motivates her students to progress, which in turn encourages their parents.

While on earth, Jesus said that the shepherd would leave the ninety-nine sheep to go after the missing one. (Luke 15:4) To go after the missing sheep involves that the good Shepherd will keep on searching for the lost sheep until He finds it. An example is that when Belle and her family were praying for Gerard's deliverance from prolonged anger toward his father, Jesus Christ went after him as a shepherd would go after a lost sheep. Eventually, Gerard gave his life over to Jesus Christ, and he had begun to mellow down. The Lord kept prompting Gerard until he made his decision. The Good Shepherd feeds us, and He protects us from all sorts of dangers.

"I shall not want." The Hebrew word for "want" means to lack, to fail, want, lessen...decrease...make lower. Since Jesus Christ is my shepherd, I shall not be in want or lack of anything, and I will not be a failure or be down and out of life. I will be in good health, have a good family life, make wise decisions, and will overcome challenges with positive results. I would have divine protection, the ability to work and be successful in my studies, business, or career. For instance, a student will be exemplary in his studies as well as his character when the Lord is his shepherd. An employee will be a blessing to his employer or an asset to that Company when the Lord is his shepherd. An employer would treat his employees with fairness when the Lord is his shepherd.

Verse Two - "He makes me lie down in green pastures" "Lie down" is a position of relaxing or resting. Life can be stressful, but when we put faith in Jesus, who is our shepherd, He puts us in a position of rest while we are in the midst of the trying situations. Jesus said, "Come to Me, all you who labor and are heavy laden, and I will give you rest." (Matthew 11:28) Stress makes us worry and panic, but this is a trick of the devil. Worry blocks peace, but peace takes away the stress. Philippians 4:6-7 encourages us that we should not be anxious about anything, but with prayer and thankfulness, God's peace will give us the confidence that we would get the desired result. First, we pray. Second, we thank God in advance for the answer to our prayers. Third, God's peace relaxes us. As the scripture says, this peace surpasses all understanding. People will not be able to comprehend how you can be calm while dealing with any challenge, but they do not know that Jesus is your good shepherd. Peace always brings victory. Note though that sometimes we may not get our prayers answered in the way we would like it too because we are limited, so we pray according to our understanding. In our finite minds, we find it may be taking a long time for God to answer our prayers; it is as if He is not doing anything. On the other hand, God is eternal, and He sees the whole picture and knows that what you asked for may not be in your best interest. In reality, He is working in the spirit realm to bring the answer to your prayers because He wants to give you something better than what you initially prayed. Another reason we sometimes wait for God to answer our prayers is that God may be prompting another person to help you. God will not force anyone to do something he does not want to do. We may have to wait for that person to act or God will prompt someone else. Nevertheless, you will get the answers to your prayers. When you receive God's best for your life, you will appreciate the wait.

Pasture is grazing land. Think of a large meadow with luscious green grass and beautiful flourishing trees. Looking at it is soothing to the eyes and refreshing to the soul. "Green pasture" is healthy grass, so that the sheep will eat to be well fed and nourished. "Green pastures" speak of the richness of God's word, the Bible. Jesus said, "It is written, 'Man shall not live by bread alone, but by every word of God." (Luke 4:4). Natural food sustains and nourishes our physical bodies, but God's Word sustains and nourishes us spiritually, which would also strengthen us emotionally, mentally, and physically to help us to be victorious through the trying times that may come against us.

When Belle was timid, she continually fed off the "green pastures." Those days she was uncertain about her performance at school and later on her job. When she understood that there is power in the written words of the Bible, she would regularly read and meditate on the scripture, then declare the word of God in her situation. One scripture Belle used often was, Philippians 4:13 "I can do all things through Christ who strengthens me." She would speak specifically to the challenge and expect to get through. She would then thank God for the answer. Belle's confidence began to grow each time she saw good results. She even got a certificate of merit for outstanding performance on one of her jobs. Belle also got Honors for a major accomplishment. Belle continues to trust God by declaring the word of God in any situation she faces. The Bible by itself is powerless. We release the power when we read and meditate on the scripture. When we speak the scripture into the situation, then we see the power of the Word of God at work.

"He leads me beside the still waters." There is a saying, "still waters run deep," which means that the stillness of the waters indicates the depth of the body of water, whether it is a lake or a river. Today this represents the Holy Spirit, who is like deep water. Jesus said in John 4:14, "But whoever drinks of the water that I shall give him will never thirst. But the water that I shall give him will become in him a fountain of water springing up into everlasting life." and at John 7:38 "He who believes in Me, as the Scripture has said, out of his heart will flow rivers of living water."

A summary of what Jesus said about the Holy Spirit in the Gospel of John. Jesus called Him "another Helper." The King James Version said "another Comforter." To live the Christian life we need help and comfort from God because we cannot live according to His will without His help." Jesus said in John 6:63 "It is the Spirit who gives life; the flesh profits nothing. The words that I speak to you are a spirit, and they are life." The words written in the Bible are the words Jesus speaks. The Holy Spirit brings to our memories these words, which will help us in any situation we face. For example, you want to get high grades on your upcoming exams, so you have been studying diligently. Your grades must be over ninety-five percent for you to get a scholarship to the University of your choice. You are a bit nervous because it is very competitive, so you pray. The Holy Spirit will remind you of a scripture text from Jesus' Sermon on the Mount at Matthew 6:25-34, which said that you must not worry about anything. He went on to say that, if God takes care of the birds and the flowers and we are more valuable than they are, He would also take care of us. Worrying cannot change the situation, so the best thing to do is trust God and relax, knowing that He will answer your prayers. This principle applies to any situation in our lives. You may think, "easier said than done," but just as with physical exercise, you need to practice regularly, and it would become easier.

In Galatians 5:16-25, the apostle Paul explained one of the ways the Holy Spirit helps us. Verses 16-17 reads, "I say then: Walk in the Spirit, and you shall not fulfill the lust of the flesh. For the flesh lusts against the Spirit, and the Spirit against the flesh; and these are contrary to one another so that you do not do the things that you wish." The Holy Spirit helps us to live right so that we will not have any desire to live in the flesh. For example, Danella dealt with self-pity from her unstable home. Sometimes, she would go into depression and feel sorry for herself. When she read the above scripture during family devotion, she understood that she was feeding the "lust of the flesh." Therefore, she prayed for God to show her how "to walk in the Spirit." She learned to rely on the Lord by speaking the scripture in her life, like, "Heavenly Father, I thank you that "the joy of the Lord is my strength. Give me Your joy because I am too sad.", "I can do all things through Christ who strengthens me"; and "Not by might, nor by power, but by Your Holy Spirit." (Zechariah 4:6) The Lord gave Danella the ability to rise about her situation until she overcame depression. Danella became a jolly person who encourages depressed people. The Holy Spirit will not force us to give up the lusts of the flesh, but as we live by the Spirit, we would desire to please God of our free will. Verses 19-21 list some of the lusts of the flesh. (John 14:16-18; 25-26, John 16:5-15, and Romans 8:1-17).

Verse Three - "He restores my soul" The soul is our mind, intellect, emotions, and will. Dealing with the pressures of life over time drains a person. We cannot go back in the past and take back our childhood, or young adulthood. We cannot go back and re-make our decisions, and we cannot change the hurts and disappointments of the past. Restoration is God's way to make up for our past mistakes, wrong decisions, or the wrong choices others made for us when we were children, whatever we lost, sicknesses, and injustice. Isaiah 61:7 tells us how God restores everything back to us. "Instead of your shame you shall have double honor, and instead of confusion they shall rejoice in their portion." (Joel 2:25-26). "Double honor" indicates that God will give us back much more and much better, in everything we lost. God would restore to us more in quality or quantity than what we had before. For example, Belle and her siblings were at a disadvantage when they were children because of the instability in their home. They could not focus on their studies at school. Even though they finished high school, their achievements were mediocre. Mediocrity in their lives went on for a few years, but the time came when they began to excel in whatever they desired. Now Belle, Becky, and Danella are exceptional women in their community and jobs. These three sisters received their "double honor" from the Lord in every area of their lives.

"He leads me in the paths of righteousness." Second Corinthians 5:21 "For He made Him who knew no sin to be sin for us, that we might become the righteousness of God in Him." God provided the way for us to become righteous. God the Father made Jesus Christ the Son to take our sins upon Him by taking our place, and He paid for it with His life, so that when we believe in what He did, we receive Jesus' righteousness instead. It is an exchange, our sins for His righteousness. Our righteousness is as filthy rags, so we need Jesus' righteousness (Isaiah 64:6). Now, with the righteousness of Jesus, we can pray with confidence to our heavenly Father in the name of Jesus Christ.

"For His name sake" means the name of Jesus Christ. Philippians 2:9-11 "Therefore God also has highly exalted Him and given Him the name which is above every name, that at the name of Jesus every knee should bow, of those in heaven, and of those on earth, and of those under the earth, and that every tongue should confess that Jesus Christ is Lord, to the glory of God the Father." Jesus was already highly exalted in heaven before He came to the earth, so why did God highly exalt Him again?

Because Jesus represented human, He died as a man, and He rose from the dead as a man. The Bible called Him the "last Adam" because Adam was the first human who fell, so Jesus Christ came as a man to represent humans, and He passed the test. (First Corinthians 15:45). There is supernatural power in the name of Jesus Christ.

Verse Four – "Yea, though I walk through the valley of the shadow of death." "The valley of the shadow of death" is when we face adversities. The trials we experience originated with the devil, and he works through circumstances to affect our health, family, finances, tragedy or he works with other people to stir up trouble. There are times when you may feel as if you will not make it because of the intensity of the pressure, but when Jesus is your Good Shepherd, you will not be afraid as to the outcome, because He is always with you, even in the low periods in life. The valleys are temporary, and they have a purpose. We develop our godly character in difficult times. The valley is where we learn to trust in God completely. We praise Him for who He is – our Protector and Deliverer. We can say something like this, "Heavenly Father, I praise and exalt You. I honor You because You love me enough to give Jesus, Your beloved Son, to die for me. You are my stronghold and my deliverer, and even though I do not know the outcome of this situation, You already have one. You are the all-powerful God, and I use the authority Jesus gave to me and declared that this matter would bow at the name of Jesus Christ! Amen." When you pray like this, your faith will get stronger. You will certainly see victory in the trying situation.

David's family did not consider him important as a boy, and later on, when Absalom overthrew him as king. That was his valley of the shadow of death – rejection, and loneliness. David learned to trust in God in those times. While he was in his valley, he gained supernatural strength, and he killed both a lion and a bear with his bare hands. Later on, he killed a giant in the presence of his king and the nation. Goliath was one of the many giants David killed. Over the years, David supernaturally won many battles. We do not like the "valleys," but they will come, and we have been through many already, so we may as well put faith in God to take us through victoriously. When we pass through the challenges of life, we will not be the same again. Instead, we will be much better off than we were before. When we look back, we will realize that we also killed some "lions, bears, and giants" in the name of Jesus.

For example, on Belle's job, she was hostess, as entertainment was part of the work. Her duties included preparing the guest lists, co-coordinating with the caterers, decorations, etc. for cocktail parties and dinner receptions. Guests commended Belle for her pleasant and professional performance, which pleased her employers and they paid her well. Belle also handled the petty cash and, as she is an honest person, the balance was correct every month. However, some of Belle's colleagues were angry at her for being good at her job and getting compliments. They began to gossip and slander about her to business associates of the Company, security officers, the cleaners, and anyone they met. Belle's colleagues wanted to tarnish her reputation. They said that she came from a struggling family and she stole from the petty cash. They also questioned her relationship with her employer, implying they were having an affair.

Hearing about the malicious remarks from her colleagues hurt Belle because they were untrue. Her employer was a married man, and they have a professional relationship. Belle is a Christian woman, and she respects the sanctity of marriage; therefore, it is against her belief to get involved in an illicit affair or to steal. The slander became stressful for her, and there were times she wanted to resign from her job, but the idea of starting over elsewhere was unthinkable. Belle thought of doing two things: she could have gossiped about her colleagues to get even at them, or she could continue to be a good employee and ignore her critics because her performance on the job would speak for her. She chose the latter.

Belle was going through a "valley of the shadow of death." but she knew the Lord is her Good Shepherd. She would pray, "Heavenly Father, You know that my colleagues are lying about me. I am asking You to clear my name from the vicious attack, because Your word said, "Vengeance is Mine, I would repay, says the Lord." (Romans 12:19) "Keep them occupied with their personal affairs that they would not have the time to cause trouble in my life, in the name of Jesus. Amen."

About one year later, Belle's co-workers who were slandering her became bitter enemies. Gossip and slander are bad traits, so if they were doing it to Belle, they also did it to each other, and it backfired. These malicious employees fought against each other to the point that they could not work together again, so they resigned. Now, Belle works with co-operative colleagues, where there is teamwork. Belle "killed" her "lions and bears" because she knows the Lord, who is her Good Shepherd. There have been many other "battles" where Belle and her family even "killed giants."

"I will fear no evil, for You are with me." The normal thing to do is panic during any trying situation, but when Jesus Christ is our Good Shepherd, we will not be afraid of any hardship because we know that He is there to guide and protect us. The devil has no power over the one who knows that the Lord is his Shepherd. He is a deceiver, and he tries to frighten us by putting lying symptoms in our path. He wants us to feel that God is not doing anything to deliver us from the problem. God can deliver someone in different ways. When fear enters our minds, is the time we must build up our faith and patience by declaring the appropriate scripture while waiting for the breakthrough to manifest.

For example, there were times when Belle felt afraid as if God was not answering her prayers when she was praying for her father to break the addiction to alcohol. The devil tried to weaken her faith by having her focus on her father's continuous bad behavior. He also tried to frighten her by using negative people to make cruel remarks about her father's bad habits, and he could not keep a job. The continuous drinking and smoking were lying symptoms from the devil. Nevertheless, she persistently prayed and declared scripture over the situation anyway until he lost the taste for alcohol and tobacco. Gradually, Ralph's behavior started changing. Belle prayed the same way for her brother, Gerard and got good results. These two incidents were only the beginning of the many obstacles Belle faced and overcame with the Lord Jesus Christ.

The devil tried to frighten Belle by throwing lying symptoms to sabotage her faith in God, but she overcame by her determination to keep trusting God for deliverance and breakthrough, which she received each time. The first lying symptom was the death of her brother, Gerard. Belle felt as if God had failed her family. Learning that the person who died in the Lord is resting with Jesus until he receives his glorified body, where there would be no more sickness and death, helped her. (2 Corinthians 5:8; Romans 6:5). The understanding of death and resurrection gave her the joy and strength to move forward. Also, it helped her to cope with the deaths of her father, sixteen years after Gerard died, and her sister, Becky, a few years her father's death. She misses them, but not with sorrow, because she has the assurance that she would meet her dead loved ones at the resurrection.

The second lying symptom was in her marriage. Belle got married young, while she was growing spiritually, one year after Gerard died. Her husband was a conniving, manipulative and greedy man. He knew Belle and her family were grieving over Gerard's death and they were vulnerable. Belle had inherited her grandparents' house, and her husband wanted it more than her, so he sent people to terrorize her on a few occasions. One time he put a scorpion in her handbag, and another time, he put a snake under the bed. He stole one of her puppies and gave him to one of his girlfriends. The above list was some of the schemes Belle's husband used against her to scare her into signing over the house. When all of the tactics her husband used against her failed. He became frustrated and began to threaten to kill her if she does not sign the house over to him. Belle was a prayerful person and knew her scripture, but she also knows that faith is an action word. She reported him to the police a few times. He told her that reporting him to the police and taking a protection order against him would not stop him from killing her. If he cannot get the house, then she cannot live there. He would rather go to prison than allow her to live in "his" house. Belle knew Proverbs 27:12, which reads, "A prudent man foresees evil and hides himself; the simple pass on and are punished." She thought to herself, "I would let wisdom prevail. I am not going to take the chance to see if he would go through with his threat." For a long time, she prayed for him to back off, but he was still around. Belle gave him the house because life is more important than anything is. She could buy another house, but she cannot buy another Belle.

Belle prayed to God for justice, because the Bible said, "all God's ways are justice. (Deuteronomy 32:4) She knows God would restore to her more than what she lost. Belle got a divorce from her husband, and in time, Belle bought a new house, which is bigger and more beautiful than the one she had before. During the stressful situation in her marriage, Belle knew that the Lord was with her. She "killed" the "giant" in her life. Years later, her ex-husband regretted his actions toward Belle, when he saw how much she has accomplished, but she had moved on, and she was not interested.

Some people felt Belle lost, but she did not lose. Belle knew that wisdom is a "weapon" to bring down "giants," just like how David killed Goliath with one stone. To King Saul and his troops, David was an insignificant young man, with five stones and a slingshot. He was not a match for a trained warrior like Goliath, but he killed the giant. In the same way, wisdom was the "stone" Belle used to get rid of her treacherous husband. She is now free from him, and he cannot hurt her. The thought of her parents getting the news that their daughter's husband murdered her was horrendous. It is better to be alive than to be murdered. Backing away from danger is being wise. Today, Belle is more successful than when she was married. She is in a position where she can help many persons. Now, Belle makes good decisions. Ralph and Frances' family learned that when one is vulnerable is not the time to make serious decisions, like marriage or money transactions.

"Your rod and Your staff they comfort me." The rod and staff are the shepherd's tools. The shepherd's rod had on one end a point to keep away predators like wolves, lions, and bears from the sheep. On the other end is a fork that was used to place over the neck of the serpent to protect the lamb from its sting. Jesus referred to the devil and his demons as serpents and scorpions. Luke 10:19 "Behold, I give you the authority to trample on serpents and scorpions, and over all the power of the enemy, and nothing shall by any means hurt you." How does this help me in my difficulty?

The staff is to guide the sheep on the right path if any stray from the fold. In life's journey, the Holy Spirit will guide us in the right direction and prevent us from going astray so we will not get hurt. For example, someone asked Becky to accompany her to the movies. She got an uncomfortable "gut" feeling about it, so she prayed to God "What is wrong? It is a good movie." Someone else reveals to her the reason for the invitation was to introduce her to a young man who wanted to meet her. That young man's character is questionable and can cause her harm, so she declined the invitation. Therefore, the Holy Spirit protected Becky from danger. God protects us numerous times, and we do not even know about it. That "gut" feeling is our intuition. The Oxford Dictionary defines "intuition" as "the ability to understand or know something immediately, without conscious reasoning." You cannot have any physical evidence of a person's motive because you do not know what goes on in his mind, but the Holy Spirit knows, and He will show you by giving you that uncomfortable "gut" feeling. The "gut" feeling is like an alarm that goes off to indicate that there is some danger. The Holy Spirit warns you, and therefore, you avoid getting hurt.

Let us look at an example of Becky, who grew up in an unstable home. When her father was drunk and enraged, he would throw things out of the house. That included clocks, the radio, food, vases, small appliances, crockery and cutlery, and anything that he was able to reach out at that moment. When Becky understood the above scripture, she recognized that demons were responsible for her father's alcoholism and bad behavior. She believed in her heart that Jesus had given her the authority over any situation, and this is how she dealt with it. "Heavenly Father, I thank You for the authority over the devil that Jesus gave me in His name. I speak to the spirit of addiction and bad behavior and command you to leave my father and never return. I declare soundness of mind and body in my father, in the name of Jesus Christ. Amen." It did not happen overnight, but with persistence, the time came when Ralph could not smell nor drink alcohol again. Within two years, the addiction was broken and destroyed from off his life for good. Shortly after, his behavior also began to change for the better.

Verse Five – "You prepare a table before me." This "table" represents a feast, which is a time of celebration. This feast is the victory from trials. We celebrate breakthrough from trials, like healing from sicknesses, passing exams with high grades, deliverance from addiction, the final payment of debts, or overcoming any other struggle. Eventually, we see the manifestation of what we had been praying. Nothing lasts forever, and challenging situations will end. God prepared a "table" for Ralph and Frances' family when they began to see their breakthroughs. As parents, Ralph and Frances were proud to see their daughters were living godly lives with success.

"In the presence of my enemies" means that the devil and those responsible for your troubles will see your breakthrough because you cannot hide your blessings. For example, when Belle's father stopped drinking alcohol and misbehaving, God prepared a table for her and her family in the presence of their enemies. Ralph's colleagues and acquaintances were not pleased and began to call him sarcastically, "priest and pastor," but that was fine. His relatives had nothing to say about him because they did not know what to say. Many people were not pleased because Ralph's family was the subject of gossip for a long time and now it was finished. Ralph, Frances, and their daughters were celebrating. When Belle rose out of her limitations to fulfill her purpose by helping many to get out of their dysfunctional state, which is blessings in the presence of her enemies.

"You anoint my head with oil" "Oil" represents God's anointing. Matthew 16:15-16 "He said to them, "But who do you say that I am?" Simon Peter answered and said, "You are the Christ, the Son of the living God." (John 20:31). The Greek word for "Christ" is "Christos" which means, "anointed, i.e., the Messiah...Christ." Jesus Christ means that Jesus is the Anointed One or the Messiah. Christ is not His surname. The anointing is God's power by the Holy Spirit. Isaiah 61:1 "The Spirit of the Lord GOD is upon Me because the LORD has anointed Me to preach good tidings to the poor; He has sent Me to heal the brokenhearted, to proclaim liberty to the captives and the opening of the prison to those who are bound." The fulfillment of this prophecy took place when Jesus was on earth. Jesus read Isaiah 61:1 at Luke 4:18-20. Jesus purpose for coming to the earth was to deliver humankind from sin and the effects of sin. The anointing is the empowerment of the Holy Spirit. When God sent the Holy Spirit to believers, He empowers us to live the Christian life successfully. Remember, Jesus took our sin and gave us His righteousness. The anointing of Jesus Christ also comes upon His believers.

The apostle John said to Christians: First John 2:20 and 27, "But you have an anointing from the

Holy One, and you know all things..." and "...
the anointing which you have received from Him
abides in you..." When we receive Jesus Christ into
our lives, we receive the same anointing that was on
Him when He was on earth. The Holy Spirit will
give us direction in our everyday lives by "speaking"
to us. We hear Him in our spirit.

An example of this is a young man named Marc,
who got through at a College in Florida to do the
aeronautical science and flight program just a few
days before orientation. His mother, Luscia, one of
Belle's cousins, and her husband Carlos had only
five days to prepare for Marc's visa and the initial
payment for the College. Usually, it takes about
four to six weeks to make the necessary preparation,
but in their case, they needed a miracle if Marc were
to reach the College in time for orientation, which
was less than one week.

Luscia became overwhelmed with the amount of
work to do in such a short time, so she decided
to pray. The Holy Spirit directed her to a familiar
scripture at Mark 16:1-4 when Mary Magdalene,
Mary the mother of James and Salome bought spices
to anoint Jesus' body as part of their ceremonial
custom. While they were on their way to Jesus'
tomb, they expressed their concern about who

would roll away the large stone for them, but when they arrived at the tomb, the stone was not there. Luscia immediately felt the peace of God and the stress left. She gained fresh strength and energy to continue. She thought to herself, "These women could not have moved away a huge boulder, so God sent an angel to do it. If God did it for Mary and her companions, then, He can do it for me too." This family saw God's hand in every step of the way. He opened doors for them with the United States Embassy, and they got the visa for Marc within two days. When they went to see about the financing for the College, they met the right person who understood their situation, and he gave them preferential treatment by releasing the funds within one day. Luscia's experience is how the anointing of the Holy Spirit works. He led Luscia to the particular scripture for her situation, which strengthened her. She listened to the "voice" of the Holy Spirit, and she got good results. The anointing of the Holy Spirit brings supernatural life to anything you put your mind to do.

"My cup runs over" means "more than enough." Our Good Shepherd gives us more than we need. He blesses us in every area of our lives, spiritually, emotionally and physically. The Good Shepherd gives us good health because Psalm 91:10 reads, "no plague will come near your dwelling" and He protects us from danger (Psalm 91:11-12). He provides for us financially by giving us the ability to work and to manage our money well. (Philippians 4:19; 2 Thessalonians 3:10). He gives us happy families, where there is love, trust, and faithfulness. (Colossians 3:18-21; Hebrews 13:4).

Ralph saw his cup running over after he received Jesus Christ in his life. The Holy Spirit overflowing in his life helped him to overcome his inadequacies. When he and his family received Jesus Christ, he saw healing, breakthrough, and restoration in abundance. In turn, Ralph and his family can help other hurting people by leading them to Jesus Christ for them to get their deliverance and breakthrough. God gives us more than enough so that we can have for ourselves and share with others.

Verse Six – "Surely goodness and mercy." When the Lord is our shepherd, God is good to us all the time, even in unfavorable circumstances. In our limited mindset, we may not feel God's goodness toward us. As explained above, adversities have a purpose in our lives. God's goodness will take us through situations with victory. He protects us from hurt while we have trouble. In the same way, just as His goodness, God's mercy is always with us. Mercy is the virtue, where God forgives us if we sin. Jesus Christ paid for our sin, so you can have the full confidence in God's goodness and mercy in your life when the Lord is your shepherd.

"Shall follow me all the days of my life." When Jesus Christ is your good Shepherd, goodness and mercy shall follow you for the rest of your life, just as how your shadow follows you. You cannot get away from goodness and mercy just as you cannot get away from your shadow. God's goodness and mercy are amazing because when you are in trouble, goodness and mercy would be there to protect and guide you. You need goodness and mercy to be with you always so that you would have a clear direction for your whole life.

"And I will dwell in the house of the LORD forever." To "dwell in the house of the LORD" is two-fold. The first meaning is to be in God's presence. The night before His crucifixion, Jesus Christ prayed for us. John 17:20-23 "...that they all may be one, as You, Father, are in Me, and I in You; that they also may be one in us just as We are one: I in them, and You in Me; that they may be made perfect in one..." Since Jesus lives in those who believe in Him, then His presence is always with us. The second meaning to "dwell in the house of the LORD" is the church.

Psalm 92:12-13 "The righteous shall flourish...in the courts of our God" The righteous establishes himself in the Lord as he worships God. The house of God or church is where we grow, flourish and bear fruit that pleases God. (Galatians 5:22-23) "Forever" is a very long time, which goes into eternity. Therefore, we will dwell in the house of the LORD in our lifetime now in this age, and later on in eternity.

Psalm 23 taught Belle and her family about trusting God in trying times and of the importance of being in His presence. Her faith in God continues to give her the victory in whatever situation she faces. She is not afraid of anything because she knows that every circumstance will bow at the name of Jesus Christ. Belle gains her knowledge from reading and meditating in the Bible, along with the experiences she gains when she sees the breakthrough. The Lord always provides for and protects her family. She learned about spiritual warfare and that God equips her to deal with an unseen enemy, the devil, whom Jesus Christ defeated on the cross. Belle is confident of always being in God's presence. She recognizes that she needs to enforce what He has already done for us. These experiences contribute to making Belle and her family better than they used to be.

CHAPTER 6

CHARACTER

E ALL WANT THE RIGHT people in our lives; this is why our choice of association is very important. Now, let us look at it from the other person's perspective; they also want the right people to be in their lives. Therefore, we should treat others the same way we would like them to treat us. (Matthew 7:12) We should be people of good character. What is our character? The Pocket Oxford English Dictionary describes the character as the qualities that make a person different from other people; strength and originality in a person's nature; and a person's good reputation. Our unique and individual personality, the way we think, speak, smile, our gesture, and our behavior, etc. shows our character. We speak what is already in our minds. Although we cannot read minds, a person's words and actions reveal his character. When our character is intact, people will respect us, and they would like to be around us.

The following points are in the form of questions to help us evaluate ourselves and to recognize what our character is like so we will see how to improve on it.

- How do I see myself?
- Am I lovable or unlovable?
- Do I like or do I hate myself?

- Am I a sensitive or touchy person?
- Am I easily offended?
- Do I overlook petty offenses?
- How do I accept compliments?
- Am I suspicious of other people's motives toward me?
- Do I give people the benefit of the doubt?
- How do I behave when things do not go my way?
- Do I snap at others when I face adversities or am I calm?
- What is my conversation mostly about – ideas, things, or people?
- Do I like to gossip?
- Do I put others down so that I can feel good about myself?
- Do I build them up, even if my conditions are not the best?
- How do I feel about another person's success?
- Am I happy for them or am I envious?
- Do I crave for what belongs to others?
- Do I boast about my accomplishments or am I modest?
- Am I sympathetic or apathetic toward hurting people?
- Do I look for faults in others or see the good in them?
- Do I only criticize or compliment?

- Am I a complainer or thankful?
- Do I tell others about someone's mistakes or shortcomings?
- Do I keep people's weaknesses to myself?
- Do I make fun of the distresses of others or show compassion to them?
- If I could cheat and get away with it, would I do it?
- Would I do the right thing because it is right, even if nobody would find out?
- Do I admire others' strengths or minimize them?
- Am I genuine or pretentious in the presence of others?
- Do I want to fit in so badly that I will compromise my values and standards?
- Do I seek the approval of those in authority by kissing up to them and bypass my peers?
- What are my feelings toward those in authority?
- What do I think about most of the time? (1) Negative thoughts or (2) Pleasant thoughts?
- Do I have set goals for my life?
- Am I working towards my goals?

Depending on how we answer these and similar questions, will show us our true character. Our behavior is the outward expression of the way we think and what we believe. For example, a man like Ralph, in chapter one, who grew up in an abusive home may think that he is not worthy and whatever he does will never be good enough. When he was a child, and even as a young adult, so many people had demeaned him. Ralph felt as if his family wounded his heart and then punished him for behaving badly. Now, as an adult, he hates his life. Because of his inadequacies, he believes that he is a failure. His frequent outbursts toward his son were a reflection of how he felt about himself. He may also have developed disrespect for authority because the adults in his life neglected him and put him down. What can this man give to his wife and children? Only what he knows, insults and ridicule.

Deep-rooted insecurity and low self-worth in a person are the reasons behind criticizing, faultfinding, belittling another person so he can look good to others, and say mean things about people behind their backs. People hide their insecurities by doing these things. Children thrive on security from their primary caregivers – parents, grandparents, guardians, teachers, and nannies. When parents' abuse children in any form – verbal, neglect, mental, sexual, or physical – it will hinder the normal growth. Abuse breaks a child's spirit, which leads to low self-worth and then he grows up and becomes a dysfunctional adult. There is hope for anyone in this position.

Romans 12:2 " And do not be conformed to this world, but be transformed by the renewing of your mind, that you may prove what *is* that good and acceptable and perfect will of God." "Conform" means to obey or follow the rules or standards; be similar in form or type. "Transform" means change or be changed in appearance, form, or nature. "Renew" is to begin again after an interruption. When we break down this scripture, it tells us that we should not follow the standards or be similar to the natural system of this world, which works through the minds of people in general. Low self-worth, envies, dishonesty, timidity, aggressiveness, immorality, and dishonesty, etc. but we should change our nature by reading and meditate on the word of God. The Holy Spirit will help us to change and become better than we are present, which will give fresh life and strength to our character. Then we will become people with high standards.

Adversities are a part of life because we live in a fallen world. (Genesis 3:1-19). The devil and his demons are responsible for all the bad things we experience, and they are relentless in their attacks against us. They work through circumstances and people. God has already intervened by making way for us to have the victory through Jesus Christ. Even though we do not like the troubles of life and God does not cause them, He uses them for our good. (Romans 8:28).

An illustration of God using unfortunate situations to our advantage is in the formation of precious and semi-precious stones. Magma, which is the very hot fluid or semi-fluid material under the earth's crust, rises to the surface of the earth. While the liquid cools, it forms into rocks. The high temperatures change the structure of the original minerals into "new kinds of minerals in the process." Just as how magma cools, when it rises from the depths of the earth to the surface, the problems we face will eventually cool down. Challenging situations can be severe, but just as with the minerals, over time, the structure would change under high pressure or temperature to produce new kinds of minerals. In like manner, the difficulties we face would change the defects in our nature into delightful qualities when we rely on God, and we would become better people than we were before. As we admire beautiful gems like diamonds, rubies, emeralds, sapphire, turquoise, amethyst, jade, jasper, onyx, and much more, people would also admire you and would like to be around you. Even if you do not say a word, your presence alone will make people happy. They would enjoy listening to you when you speak. No matter what they are dealing with, whenever they are around you, they would be encouraged as not to give up.

These gems are not only beautiful, but they are expensive. God's blessings in your life are free to you, but it cost Jesus Christ His life, which is very expensive. Jesus Christ faced a brutal death, which He did not deserve. He suffered and died to give us a good life – everlasting life. First Peter 1:18-19 "Knowing that you were not redeemed with corruptible things, as silver or gold but with the precious blood of Christ, as of a lamb without blemish and without spot." Gold and silver are precious metals, but compared with the "blood of Christ" they are corruptible because they are in creation but Christ is the Creator. You will become a blessing to those you meet. Just as how the beautiful gems have a positive effect on its viewers, this is how God works all things out for our good; you too will have a positive effect on your peers. You will become a better person than you were before.

One of the best examples in the Bible of character transformation is a Canaanite prostitute named

Rahab from the city of Jericho. The events took place in the book of Joshua 2 and 6:17, 22-23, 25; and Hebrews 11:31. Rehab, being a prostitute, was common and normal to the Canaanites because they were pagan worshippers. Their worship involved the high places where they prayed to gods and goddesses. Cult practices, child sacrifices, and sexual immorality, like orgies, homosexuality, and multiple partners, etc. were some of the practices, which took place. Male and female temple prostitutes were also a part of pagan worship; therefore, their lifestyle also reflected it.

All the Canaanites heard about what God had done for the Israelites at the Red Sea and during the forty years, the time they spent in the wilderness, and how God had provided for and protected them. (Joshua 2:9-11) Only Rahab had faith in God. Joshua, the chief commander of Israel, sent two of his warriors to spy out the land. Rahab helped the Israelite spies by hiding them from the soldiers of Jericho in Canaan. Therefore, God spared her, along with her family, when He destroyed Jericho. From then on, she lived with the Israelites and began to worship God. Rahab's life changed, which altered the course of her descendants' lives forever, and she was never a prostitute again. She gave up pagan worship with its perverted practices to worship the God of the Israelites. She got married to a good Israelite named Salmon. She became the great-grandmother of King David, who was an ancestor of Jesus Christ. Rahab, an ex-prostitute, is an ancestress of Jesus Christ and her name is on the list of Jesus Christ's ancestors. (Matthew 1:5). Rahab moved from someone with a promiscuous reputation to a virtuous woman of honor and dignity. She became the first generation in her family to break the generational curse of centuries to a generational blessing for her descendants. You can also read about Rahab's marvelous son Boaz, who was an honorable man, who got married to another amazing woman from a foreign country, Moab, named Ruth. Just as the Canaanites, the Moabites were pagan worshippers and their worship involved human sacrifices, lustful orgies, and wanton rites. Read about how Ruth's right choice led her to Boaz, in the book of Ruth.

God is the only Judge; therefore, we should not label anyone as hopeless because of his deficiencies. God alone knows what is in a person's heart and mind. On the surface, people would have seen a prostitute by the name of Rahab, but God saw Rahab's excitement about the Israelites crossing the Red Sea on dry ground. He saw her reaction when she heard about the Israelite's defeating enemy nations during their trek in the wilderness. (Deuteronomy 20:15-18) Rahab's heart gravitated toward God when she heard that the Israelites did not starve as God had provided for them. It took the Israelites forty years from the crossing of the Red Sea to the crossing of the Jordan River to enter into Jericho. Rahab's faith in God did not happen suddenly. It was building up with every good news she heard because she knew that God helped the Israelites each step of the way. The Bible did not give Rahab's age, but to be a prostitute, she had to have been a young woman. Maybe she had not even been born forty years earlier when the Israelites crossed the Red Sea. Nevertheless, she would have been hearing talk around her about the God of the Israelites, and what He did for His people.

For a long time, Rahab probably prayed secretly to the God of the Israelites to give her a life with meaning and purpose. God heard her prayers and answered them. Even though she was a prostitute, does not mean she liked her profession. She may have thought, "The God of the Israelites is mighty and powerful. I want Him to be my God." She took the opportunity to show her faith in God when the Israelite spies entered Jericho. No one knew that faith was building up in Rahab's heart over the years, but God did. God maneuvered circumstances to save Rahab and change her life. What happened to Rahab was not a behavior modification; where she changed her life through her ability. It was a heart transformation by the Holy Spirit.

Today, you may have come from a dysfunctional background, or maybe you have been a victim of injustice and developed flaws in your character. Do not allow anyone to label you as "nobody" or "loser." If you have faith in Jesus Christ, He will deliver you from all defects and replace them with His virtues, which will give you a good character. Romans 10:13 "For "whoever calls on the name of the Lord shall be saved." "Saved" in the original Greek, means "heal, preserve, save, do well, be (make) whole." (Acts 2:21; Romans 10:9) Therefore, salvation is more than deliverance from going to hell, but it involves healing and deliverance from hurts, among physical healing and deliverance from personality defects. Call on Jesus, and He will deliver you from anything that is holding you back from progressing and living successfully. Just like Rahab, you would get a heart transformation, which would make you into a better person than before.

Frances mentioned in chapter one is a modern day example of character transformation. She was timid and embarrassed as a child with her mother then later with her husband. People knew her to be quiet and felt sorry for her. When she gave her life to the Lord Jesus Christ, she learned how to trust in God during the trying times. She saw this scripture in Isaiah 43:2 and 19 "When you pass through the waters, I will be with you; and through the rivers, they shall not overflow you. When you walk through the fire, you shall not be burned, nor shall the flame scorch you. Behold, I will do a new thing, now it shall spring forth; shall you not know it? I will even make a road in the wilderness and rivers in the desert." She prayed like this, "Heavenly Father, You promised me in Your word that the problem I am facing will not overwhelm me and that You will make a way out of this impossible situation even though I cannot find a way out. Thank You for delivering my family and me in Jesus' name. Amen." While she was waiting for the answer to her prayers, she continually thanked God for the answer, and she began to develop a very warm and pleasant personality, along with boldness and assertiveness. This pleasantness attracted people to her, especially younger women. She was able to guide them to the Lord as well as give practical advice on everyday matters. Nobody feels sorry for Frances anymore. She moved from being timid and quiet to be a source of strength. Most of her friends today are younger women than her. Some of them are young enough to be her daughters and granddaughters. Just as the illustration of the formation of precious gems, the adversities in Frances' life changed her into an amazing person, where she helps many persons.

Both Ralph and Frances experienced insults and ridicule as children and as young adults due to their unstable condition. One instance had to do with their son, Gerard. Gerard did not know how to socialize with other children and later on with people, because of the continuous verbal abuse from his father, along with a mental condition. No one laughs at physical sicknesses, but many persons would laugh at mental illnesses because of the strange behavior of the individual. People can be cruel, and both children and adults used to make fun of him by calling him names, like "ghost," "dumb," "loony," etc. These callous remarks deeply hurt Gerard and his family. At that time, they were still in a dysfunctional state, and they did not know how to handle the situation, so they went through life feeling bad. Therefore, over the years, while they were overcoming their challenges, they developed compassion toward people in their distress. Ralph and Frances passed this good quality down to their daughters, Belle, Becky, and Danella. Their three daughters grew up to be women of godly character and were able to overcome their shortcomings. Their warm personality and positive outlook on life attract sincere persons.

Like everything in life, there will be critics and faultfinders, but they do not know of your struggles, when you were dealing with low self-worth, lack of confidence, and insecurities, etc. Your critics do not know how many times you sought God for deliverance and breakthrough. Your faultfinders do not know about the process of character building taking place within your soul while waiting for the desired results. The foundation for character building is accepting God's unconditional love for you and loving yourself. God's love provided the way for a complete breakthrough from all our shortcomings through Jesus Christ. Just as how no one sees the molten rock cooling down because of it under the earth's crust, in the same way, no one sees the formation of your character because it is internal.

For Belle, the process of character building involved forgiving her grandmother and her uncles, for being cruel to her father, since he was a child. Their insults continued into his adulthood, but Belle kept a good attitude toward them by being respectful. Even though her father was still an alcoholic, jobless, and verbally abusive, she would continue to pray for him to change. Jesus said that when we pray in secret, God will reward us openly (Matthew 6:6). In Belle's situation, building a good character also included forgiving the people who mocked Gerard when he could not help himself to be a loner. The process also involved showing kindness and compassion to the suffering, while she was hurting and nobody knew. Even though Belle had some bad experiences with deceitful people, she would be sincere to those around her.

Just as how newly formed gemstones are rough and dull, so gem cutters must cut, grind and polish the gemstones to make them shine, in the same way, faultfinders are like the process of cutting, grinding and polishing, which is an unpleasant feeling, but the result is a beautiful warm personality. These processes take time, so many times, ten, fifteen, and twenty years later, another generation, who were not born when you were dealing with your troubles, would benefit from your blessings.

Your critics and faultfinders would see your blessings and would give their negative opinion about your successes without knowing all the facts. Even those who knew you when you had your problems may criticize you because of jealousy when they see how far you have reached and how successful you have become, but they would not compliment you. They do not know what dedication and sacrifices it took you to reach where you are today. You did without many things during your struggles and did not complain. Now, you are enjoying the reward of your diligence.

If only your faultfinders would recognize there is no need to be envious because we were all born with God-given talents and gifts, which will bless many. They would find peace and enjoy their lives. Do not allow them to steal your joy and peace because they are insecure and unhappy people who are dissatisfied with their lives. Do not waste your energy on miserable people, as they intend to sidetrack you from your purpose. Your part is to ignore them and continue to trust in God to be your best, and He would do great things through you. You will become a living testimony as to the goodness of God. Your good character will cause you to behave in a dignified manner toward your critics, which, in turn, will make you sparkle more, like beautiful gemstones. Many people would benefit from your God-given gifts and talents. They would admire and approve of you. When you look at an authentic and sparkling diamond necklace, a pair of beautiful ruby earrings, a breathtaking emerald bracelet set in gold, or a stunning sapphire ring, you do not think of the unshaped, liquefied molten rocks or the dull colorful stones they used to be. You see the finished work of the beautiful jewelry, and you enjoy them. It is the same way people will see you as authentic and enjoy your company. In the past, it hurt Belle when anyone minimized her efforts or brought up her family's past. Today faultfinding and criticism do not affect her. Belle has a vague memory of how boredom and frustration feel. Her experiences of God's love and grace toward her family exceed her expectations, and it gives her joy.

Belle and her sisters know what they had been through and how God delivered them and transformed their lives. Today, they are glittering and sparkling, like the beautiful gemstones. They moved from being insecure and having low self-worth to being confident and competent. These women are now in a position to add value to those they meet. Their satisfaction is in helping others to become better people than they are at present.

People's opinion of Belle does not intimidate her anymore because she knows that her security is in Jesus Christ, which gives her the strength to stand up courageously to any opposition that may come against her and overcome them. A secure person always lifts others up and not put them down. She knows her Bible well, how to pray effectively, and how to conduct herself with propriety. The anointing of the Holy Spirit on her life gives her the ability to encourage the people she meets. One example of this is at her local church. Belle goes to every church service one hour earlier to greet church members when they arrive. She sincerely makes each person feel as if he/she is the most important person in the world. One cancer patient, in particular, looks forward to her greetings because while she is waiting for the manifestation of her healing, Belle's anointing words encourage her not to give up hope to be healthy again.

Becky was a prayer warrior. When she prayed, you would feel the anointing of the Holy Spirit moving, and she gets good results. She prayed according to the Word of God. For example, there was a thoughtless neighbor, named Jeff, who used to play his music so loud that Becky's family could not hear the television or listen to anything on youtube. She politely asks him to put down the volume, but he was rude and ignored her. She told his mother about Jeff playing loud music, and she snapped at Becky, saying, "he is a young man, leave him alone!" Becky called the police, and they spoke with the young man, but he continued anyway. Becky decided to pray about the matter, "Heavenly Father, thank You for the authority Jesus Christ gave me in His name. I command the stubborn spirit in Jeff to leave now, and I declare that he will put the volume of his music down, in the name of Jesus. Amen." About twenty minutes later, Jeff lowered the volume in his music. Behind the scenes, unknown to Becky at the time, Jeff's mother got a headache, as the music was too loud and she asked him to turn it down. After about two months of Jeff's loud music and his mother's complaints about getting headaches, he moved out of the area.

Jeff and his mother are an example of how selfish some people could be. True, Jeff is a young man and he could enjoy his music with his friends. However, that does not give him the right to infringe on the comforts of others. There are people of all ages in the world; the elderly, the young, babies, and the sick, so parents should teach their children at an early age to show respect and consider how their actions would affect others.

Danella has a gift for young children. She belongs to a women's group with outreach to help victims of child abuse and women who are victims of domestic violence. Children would meet Danella for the first time and like her. She can relate to them, and in turn, they find it easy to talk to her. Shortly after meeting, Danella would encourage parents and children with Scripture from the Bible and share motivational quotes. As a pre-school teacher, Danella uses effective methods to teach her students. She sees more than a classroom; she sees individual children who are unique and works with them to bring out the best. All the parents commend her for the excellent work she does with their young children.

Danella recently had a wonderful experience with one of her students. A four-year-old girl named Nellie belongs to a non-believing home. Nellie goes to a Christian pre-school and learns about Jesus. She would speak about Jesus Christ at home, but her family was not interested, as they see her as just a little girl who is babbling some fairy tale. One day, her grandmother got a heart attack at home. While the family was frantically waiting for the ambulance to arrive, Nellie put her hand on her grandmother's head and prayed, "Heavenly Father, make Mama well. Heal her in the name of Jesus Christ." Nellie's uncle shouted, "Move this child away!" Then grandma sat up and said, "Do not shout, you are giving me a headache." Shortly after, the ambulance arrived and took her to the hospital. All the tests in the hospital showed that grandma had a mild heart attack, but she was doing well. The hospital gave her medication and referred her to the heart clinic. Of course, the family was relieved to see their mother doing well. Nellie spoke up and said, "Jesus healed Mama." Everyone in the room realized that it was after Nellie had prayed for her Mama that she got up from the bed. Most of the members of this family are now going to church to learn about Jesus.

Good parenting is also necessary for developing good character in children. Proverbs 22:6 "Train up a child in the way he should go, and when he is old he will not depart from it." Training involves teaching and setting good examples. Parents are to direct their children on the right path. By the time a child becomes a teenager, he should be able to make good decisions, even when his parents are not around. Psalm 119:9, 11 "How can a young man cleanse his way? By taking heed according to your word. Your word I have hidden in my heart, that I might not sin against You." A youth hides God's Word in his heart by reading and meditating on the scripture.

For example, a young Christian woman named Trishana is from a good Christian family with high values. She is a medical student in a foreign country, and she belongs to a study group. She is exemplary and outstanding in her demeanor. Some of the people in her study group do not share her beliefs, as their values are different from hers. Some of them are dishonest, they live in sexual immorality, smoke cigarettes, take drugs, lie, cheat, use obscene language, etc. and there are those who may not even believe in God.

On Friday evenings, her peers from the group go out together, but she keeps away because she is familiar with this scripture at Proverbs 22:3, A prudent man foresees evil and hides himself, but the simple pass on and are punished." Trishana would meditate or think carefully about this verse, so she will look into the Bible Concordance or the dictionary to get the meaning of the word "prudent." Prudent is to think about the future. Therefore, Proverbs 22:3 tells us that a prudent person is wise, sensible and far-sighted. This person has the foresight to consequences and is cautious before he takes action. Trishana understands this scripture well so she reasons with herself, "A lot of things could go wrong if I go out with this group because their activities are not to my taste, and I do not want their negativity to affect me. It is better for me to limit my association with them to studying only. It is wise and sensible for me to protect myself from potential harm." Therefore, she uses prudence by carefully thinking about the repercussions. She reasons that it would be better to prevent something bad from happening than to get hurt and regret it later. Instead, she would go out with other students with high values, and they would have fun and decently enjoy themselves. On the other hand, those students she goes out with would benefit from being around her as she motivates them to rise higher. Medical science has made a lot of breakthrough over the decades, and we are thankful, but they are still limited because they can only manage the symptoms, but not cure them. One of Trishana's goals is to find cures for at least one of the critical illnesses, like mental disorders, high blood pressure, high cholesterol, diabetes, cancer, or even the common cold, etc. Their conversation would be uplifting and beneficial. She is a good friend, someone with a good character. She knew to choose that scripture verse, Proverbs 22:3 for this situation because she is accustomed to reading and meditating on her Bible.

Along with parents, early childhood teachers contribute to instilling high ideals in young children. Pre-school teachers assist parents in laying foundations in their children's lives. The principal, Miss Nicole, at the school where Danella teaches is a professional woman with good character. Her family has a good reputation in the community in which she lives. Miss Nicole sets a high standard in education as well as life skills. She believes that education is more than learning the alphabet, spelling, being able to read, counting, writing, and unstructured play. Life skills are a part of the school structure; like teaching the young ones about ethics, decorum, and teamwork. She upholds high values and, therefore, teaches it to her young students. Secular education and play are important and necessary for growth, but without values, children grow up to be talented and highly educated, yet full of attitude, snobbish, and disrespectful, along with the bad habits they develop over the years. The age group of these children is between three and five years old. She knows that young children's minds take in everything they see and hear. Therefore, she gives her young students lessons in good manners and values at the appropriate age level.

Like parents, early childhood teachers have a great responsibility in helping the little ones to become people of character. Building character in toddlers involves patiently teaching them to get along well with each other by showing them how. As a Christian woman, Miss Nicole knows her scripture well. Deuteronomy 6:6-7 "And these words which I command you today shall be in your heart. You shall teach them diligently to your children, and shall talk to them when you sit in your house, when you walk by the way, when you lie down, and when you rise." This scripture is primarily for parents, but it can also apply to teachers, as they contribute in instilling values into their students. Since children learn by example, they imitate their teachers' kind and caring behavior. Children imitate the respect, courtesy, and co-operation among their teachers.

Since the school environment is one for learning, discipline is a major part of the process. Many people think discipline is just punishment, but according to The Oxford Dictionary, discipline means "the training of people to obey rules or code of behavior." Therefore, training involves repetition, practical participation, and timeout when necessary for misbehaving and interrupting the class. With godly wisdom, Miss Nicole trains her young students through secular education and high ideals.

For Miss Nicole to accomplish her work effectively, she employs competent teachers, who will uphold her high standards. Although there are many qualified teachers, she wisely selects teachers who hold the same high values as she. Miss Nicole does not condone gossip and competition among her teachers, as this can disrupt the professional status and peace of the school. The purpose of maintaining unity among the teachers is to lay a solid foundation for their young students. Children are impressionable, and they take in everything they see and hear. Therefore, for teachers to impart high values to their students, they first need to have it in themselves.

Miss Nicole and her teachers greet each parent with pleasantries as he/she arrives at school with his/her child. There are two reasons for greeting parents. (1) Parents feel comfortable with the pleasant greetings from their children's teachers because it assures them that their children are safe. (2) We do not know what challenges parents are dealing with at home or on the job, so a kind word can be a boost to their morale to face the day.

The school day begins with assembly, where the children pray, sing the national anthem, and sing nursery rhymes, and Sunday school songs to help them learn the Bible. An assembly is also a place when the young students learn to listen to their teachers and follow instructions. Miss Nicole teaches the children to go to their classrooms in an orderly manner to learn their secular work. Later on in the day, they learn about good manners and behavior, hygiene, values like telling the truth, honesty, like do not steal and lie, share their crayons and building blocks with their peers, and fighting is unacceptable, etc. The young students look forward to story and drama. The teachers, along with the class dramatize familiar stories, like "The Three Little Pigs," "Jack and the Beanstalk," and "Little Red Riding Hood," etc. There is some time each week for teacher/student interaction, where the children are free to express their concerns and their ideas. In turn, the teacher would give her input and direction to her class. During this time, children learn to show respect to their parents and teachers, nobody must touch them inappropriately, and that they should not talk to strangers. The students' favorite is song and dance. They would sing and dance to pre-school songs on Youtube.

An important factor is that the teachers say to their students, "I am proud of you" or "good work" whenever they hold the crayons properly and trace their names or make an effort to spell two and three letter words. A child feels so good when a teacher or parent commends him, as he flourishes with acceptance so he will aim to please his primary caregivers. The students will make every effort to please Miss Nicole and their teachers.

One outstanding teacher is the amazing Miss Marlene who is a beautiful person. Her demeanor is outstanding. She uses discretion with her colleagues and the parents of her students as she upholds her Christian values. Miss Marlene uses her warmth, patience, and kindness to impart secular education, as well as Christian principles in her young students. She has a gift of balancing firmness and gentleness with the children. She is firm enough without being harsh so they will respect her, but also gentle so they can go to her with any problem. When a child misbehaves, he gets "time out" so he would realize he did something wrong, which is part of discipline. When he apologizes, he goes back to his seat to continue his activity with his classmates. When he does something good, she will commend him.

To many persons, these women are just pre-school teachers, who teach toddlers the alphabet and to count from one to ten, color, play with building blocks, play dough, and do crafts. There is no such thing as "just" pre-school teachers. Children come from various backgrounds, and they come to school with their traits. No one knows what some children experience at home. Some families are living in turmoil, while others are struggling financially, and there are those who are victims of some form of abuse. Many of these toddlers continuously see and hear immoral behavior and obscenities, which can warp their young minds.

Bad behavior in the little ones is evidence that they are hurting. When parents create a stable home environment for their children, they will thrive in school and life. On the other hand, when children are living in an unstable home environment, where parents fight in their presence, it traumatizes and distresses the little ones, as they think it is their fault. The result is that it negatively affects them emotionally, which would manifest as bad behavior and poor results in school. Another factor that causes a child to misbehave is a mental disorder. In recent years, health professionals recognize that brain disorders such as bipolar disorder, anxiety disorders, or even depression can begin in early childhood. There is professional help available for the little ones who are struggling with mental disorders.

Pre-school teachers show sincere concern for their young students and show impartial warmth and fondness toward them. Teachers lay the foundation in the lives of their students, the same way a contractor would put down the foundation before putting up the structure of a building. Primary and secondary schools build on what pre-school teachers laid in the early lives of children. Authors, journalists, architects, pilots, doctors, judges, fashion designers, contractors, mechanics, and entrepreneurs, etc. were three and four years old at one time, but today they are successful business people. We cannot leave out leaders of countries as they too were toddlers many years ago.

Young students look up to their teachers and see them like queens. These teachers make school enjoyable for toddlers. Therefore, later on in primary and secondary schools, they would enjoy learning and do well.

Some children are from stable homes, where there is love, affection, and unity. I would briefly mention four of them, although there are more. First, there is a little three-year-old girl, named Gabriella. She is a happy child with loving and upright parents, who sets good examples for her to follow. Gabriella is bright, and she would do her work quickly so she could talk to her teacher during class. She addresses her teacher as "my Miss" because she believes that "Miss" is her "personal" teacher. She is young, and she would learn that "Miss" is the teacher of the whole class and that there is a time for everything. Second, there is another three-year-old little girl, named Myah. She is a happy child, with loving and upstanding parents and an amazing grandmother, named "Mama," who is a woman of good character. Myah is bright, and she believes that she is "the boss." She loves to dance; she dances during assembly, when she is singing the alphabet, and counting from one to ten, while coloring in her coloring book, etc. On Myah's second day at school, the teacher told her that she should not dance and eat lunch at the same time. Myah threatened her teacher to call her "police mommy" to lock up Miss. Her teacher fondly calls her "my little pixie."

Third, there is a little three-year-old boy, named Ezra. He is a charming boy, who is quiet and does not talk much. His parents are decent and modest people, who shower their children with love and affection. Ezra is a bright boy who colors neatly, and he knows his alphabet well. He loves to sing and dance. One day, about three months in the school, Ezra surprised the class during song and dance. He danced up a storm that his friend, Myah, shouted out, "Ezra! You dance so nicely!" Ezra was bubbling over with excitement. During story and drama, he participates with enthusiasm. He continues to show that enthusiasm throughout the interaction, story/drama, and song and dance. Fourth, there is another charming three-year-old boy, named Nikolai. He is from a high-principled and loving family. Nikolai is very bright and fun loving. When you meet him, you want to cuddle him. He is on top of his class with saying his alphabet, counting, drawing, and coloring. He is brave and outspoken with a pleasant voice, as he speaks properly. Nikolai likes to debate. He would keep on asking a question until he gets a satisfying answer. Like the other children, he is young and mischievous at times. Nevertheless, they are learning. Good character is already developing in these young minds.

The time would come when these children would move on to primary and secondary schools. They may forget most things you said to them, but they will always remember that you made them feel as if they were worthy of love, acceptance, and appreciation. These young ones would feel as if they can attain their highest potential. By doing this, the teachers build self-worth in the children. Pre-school teachers should be kind to children, so they would turn out to be upstanding adults in society. Twenty and thirty years later, when they are successful adults, you would be proud to know that you contributed by imparting to the foundation in that person's life. One day, some of them may even want to meet and thank you for making them feel as if they could have accomplished anything they wanted to do, and they did it. You would get so much satisfaction to know that it was well worth it.

When parents pick up their children after school, the teachers send the children off with a warm smile. Parents of these children compliment Miss Nicole and her teachers for the tremendous work they are doing with their children.

Your character speaks for you. You will not have to boast about your talents or qualifications to anyone. When you do what comes naturally and joyfully, you will shine. Remember, precious gems sparkle silently; they cannot do anything else, but shine. Isaiah 60:1 "Arise, shine; for your light has come! And the glory of the LORD rises upon you. " God's glory upon your life will make you shine.

CHAPTER 7

THE BEST FRIEND

C HAPTER 1 BEGAN WITH AN illustration of laying a foundation according to the building code before putting up a house. This chapter begins with the person who is the solid foundation of our lives, Jesus Christ; we then build our lives on Him. (First Corinthians 3:11) Jesus Christ has the power and the willingness to transform our lives and make us into the best that we can become. When Jesus was on earth, He moved around with the common and oppressed people who had many problems. Jesus always had a positive impact on those He met, and He changed their lives forever. The sick got their healing, He delivered the demon-possessed, the prostitutes changed their profession from a life of lasciviousness to one of dignity, the cheating tax collector returned what he stole with interest, and he became honest, and the outcast fitted into society again. (Luke 4:40; Matthew 8:16, 28; Luke 7:37-39; John 4; Mark 1:4-41). Jesus always had a life-transforming effect on people's lives. They never affected him.

We will look at two of those persons whom Jesus transformed after they met him. The first one is at Luke 19:1-8, we read about a man named, Zacchaeus. He was a chief tax collector. He was an Israelite who worked for the Roman government to collect taxes. The tax collectors falsified documents to take more money from the oppressed people than what the law required. In those days, tax collectors used to extort money from the common people and therefore they had no respect for them. One day, Jesus was passing by the neighborhood of a chief tax collector named, Zacchaeus. He was a short man, and he could not see Jesus because of the crowd, so he climbed a tree to see Him. Jesus was popular, so when Zacchaeus heard that He was passing by, he wanted to see who He was. He may have thought, "This man is having a great impact on the lives of many. He is healing the sick and casting demons out of people. I want to see Him, but the crowd is blocking me. I will run ahead and climb the sycamore tree to get a clear view of Him."

Verse 5 reads, "And when Jesus came to the place, He looked up and saw him, and said to him, "Zacchaeus, make haste and come down, for today I must stay at your house." "Make haste" is to hurry. Jesus told Zacchaeus to hurry and come down from the tree. Verse 6 reads, "So he made haste and came down, and received Him joyfully." Zacchaeus was happy to have Jesus over at his home. Zacchaeus' excitement indicated that he was searching for something meaningful in his life for some time and he felt Jesus had the answer. The

Bible did not reveal their conversation. When Jesus went to his house, He would have shared some insightful words with Zacchaeus and his household. Whatever they discussed had a tremendous effect on Zacchaeus' life that he decided to give up his life of cheating his fellowmen. Zacchaeus gave his life to the Lord, and his thinking changed, therefore his life changed. Verse eight reads, "Then Zacchaeus stood and said to the Lord, "Look, Lord, I give half of my goods to the poor; and if I have taken anything from anyone by false accusation, I restore fourfold." These words show us that after Jesus called Zacchaeus and He spent time with him, he changed from being a cheat to an honest man.

Those on the outside did not know the facts behind Jesus going to Zacchaeus' home. Verse 7 reads, "But when they saw it, they all complained, saying, "He has gone to be a guest with a man who is a sinner." Many persons in the crowds felt that Jesus should not have gone to Zacchaeus' house because he was an extortioner. In other words, the onlookers were gossiping about Jesus' visit to the house of a chief tax collector. People who gossip lack vision and insight, as they focus only on the surface of any situation. Instead of looking at their shortcomings, they would rather see the faults of others. Each person has the potential to become a good person. It takes an insightful person to draw it out and a willing individual to co-operate. Jesus Christ is the person who can bring out a person's potential, and He did.

No one can see people's hearts or the motive behind what they do and why. No one can understand why a person like Zacchaeus, who cheated the common people, would be interested in Jesus. Jesus knew what was in Zacchaeus' heart. Jesus saw beyond his cheating and stealing into the potential of him becoming an honest man. No one has the right to judge others because of his mistakes or wrong choices. We do not know when a person may respond to Jesus' calling on his life, which would transform him.

The second person whom Jesus transformed is a woman from a town called Samaria. Let us see how the meeting with Jesus changed her life. John 4 gives us the account of the conversation between Jesus Christ and the woman at the well. The women of the town would fetch water early in the morning when the temperature was cool, but the Samaritan woman came to fetch her water when the midday sun was scorching hot at that time. She did not want to be the center of gossip so she would rather deal with the sweltering heat than to meet with the women. She probably had something to hide. She did not expect to meet anyone at the well, but she saw Jesus sitting. At that time, the Jews and the Samaritans were not friendly, even more so, men looked down at women, so she was surprised when Jesus, a Jewish man, spoke to her, a Samaritan woman. It was unheard of for a Jewish man to speak with a Samaritan woman and Jesus asked her for a drink of water. In verse 10, Jesus told her, "..."If you knew the gift of God, and who it is who says to you, 'Give Me a drink,' you would have asked Him, and He would have given you living water." Jesus said, "If you knew the gift of God." What is the gift of God? The Bible interprets scripture. Romans 6:23 "...the gift of God is eternal life in Christ Jesus our Lord." Jesus was telling the woman about salvation. He went on to tell her that He would give her "living water." Jesus did not say that He was the living water, but He would give her "living water," which means He would give her the Holy Spirit (John 7:37-39). The Samaritan woman did not yet understand that Jesus was talking about salvation and that He would give her the Holy Spirit. She thought He meant literal water to drink. She then asked Jesus to give her the water to drink that she would not get thirsty again. Then the conversation took a turn from drinking water to her personal life.

In verse 16, "Jesus said to her, "Go, call your husband, and come here." She told him that she did not have a husband and Jesus revealed to her that she had five husbands and the man she was living with was not her husband. By then, the woman thought that Jesus was a prophet. He told her about her immoral lifestyle, which was the reason she avoided the gossiping women of her town. The only difference was that Jesus did not judge her nor did He rebuke her. Jesus Christ knows our hearts – the reason we do what we do and why. It is not our place to judge and criticize others, no matter their situation. We do not know all the facts why a person is a certain way. Maybe this Samaritan woman was in the situation because of unfortunate circumstances. Back then, a woman could not apply for a divorce from her abusive husband, but the man could. Women did not have jobs to provide for their household, so prostitution or living in sexual immorality was a way for her to make a living. We do not know, so we will not judge anyone. Jesus said in Matthew 7:1-2 "Judge not, that you be not judged. ² For with what judgment you judge, you will be judged; and with the measure you use, it will be measured back to you." Jesus said that if you judge and criticize anyone, others would also judge and criticize you and you will be hurt. Think about the feelings of other people. Jesus and the woman continued to talk about worship and the Messiah to come. In verse 26, Jesus declared to her that He was the promised Messiah or Christ.

Imagine how thrilled this woman was to meet the Messiah. She may have thought to herself, "For millennia, prophets, kings, and many people waited for the coming of the Messiah. He is the One to deliver us from oppression. Here He is in person, speaking to a woman like me. What a privilege! He did not rebuke me for my lifestyle as the religious leaders; instead, He treated me with dignity. No one has ever shown me respect before. The Messiah is here talking to me, and He offered me salvation. O, my God, what an amazing Man!" She left her water pot and ran off to tell the people of her town that she met the Messiah. She did not want to hide anymore. She changed from being ashamed and shy to be bold and brave. Verses 39-42 read, "And many of the Samaritans of that city believed in Him because of the word of the woman who testified, "He told me all that I ever did." So when the Samaritans had come to Him, they urged Him to stay with them; and He stayed there two days. And much more believed because of His word. Then they said to the woman, "Now we believe, not because of what you said, for we have heard Him and we know that this is indeed the Christ, the Savior of the world." The Samaritan woman became the first evangelizer to her town.

Did you see what happened? Jesus had a positive effect on this woman's life. He was the only one to judge and rebuke her, even punish her, but He did not. Jesus said, "For God did not send His Son into the world to condemn the world, but that the world through Him might be saved." (John 3:17) Instead, He offered her salvation. Salvation is the means through which we get deliverance from sin and its effect. If Jesus were in the saving business, then we would be out of place to judge and condemn others. Normally, religious and pious people would be snobbish toward someone like her, but what they overlook is that every person has a fault. It may not be the same immoral lifestyle as hers. Nobody knows what goes on in the minds of people. The sins of the mind, which the public cannot see, are greed and jealousy, bitterness and malice, prejudice and lusts, etc. Some religious people commit the sins of the mind, but they will come against an immoral or drunk person. Even Jesus' disciples were shocked to see Jesus talking to the woman, but they did not say anything. Humans are limited, and we see the external appearances, but God sees the heart and mind. (First Samuel 16:7) Jesus Christ, the Messiah, helped this woman to change from being immoral to be respectful and dignified. Jesus Christ does not condone sin, but He came to take away our sin and give us the opportunity to accept the salvation that He offers. By continually criticizing and putting people down, would not make them better. They already know that they are doing the wrong thing, but they do not know how to get off a bad situation. Jesus Christ came to change us by His love and acceptance, which will cause us to become better people when we receive His righteousness. We need to love and accept people and allow God to do His work in their lives.

Jesus met many more persons, whose lives He transformed from being meaningless to become godly, with a purpose in life. There are Jesus' twelve disciples and others who followed Him, Mary Magdalene and the women who were His friends. Martha, Mary, and Lazarus were good friends of Jesus. If we were to interview these people today, they would give us testimonies as to how Jesus transformed their lives. Jesus did not yet die for the sin of the world when He lived on earth, but He had such a powerful effect on those He met. We live in the time post-crucifixion and resurrection, so today, we have a better opportunity than they had. Hebrews 13:8 "Jesus Christ is the same yesterday, today, and forever." He transformed lives when He was on earth, and He continues to do the same today. Jesus Christ is not like any person you know because He is our Creator. He treats women with honor, the underprivileged with dignity, and the dysfunctional with respect. Psalm 103:4 "... Who crowns you with lovingkindness and tender mercies". Royalty wears crowns, like kings, queens, princes, and princesses, etc. (First Peter 2:9-10) Jesus Christ raises us up and puts us on thrones. Today, Jesus Christ wants to make us into better people than we are present. If He healed and delivered people in the past, He would continue to do it today. At John 15:15 Jesus called us His friends. He is the best friend we can have. There will be no disappointment or injustice with Him.

The first part of Proverbs 13:20 reads, "He who walks with wise men will be wise." "Walk" means what we do in our everyday life. Proverbs 8:12-31 refers to Jesus Christ as the person of Wisdom. Adam and Eve did a foolish act in the Garden of Eden, and humans are still paying for it today. We inherited the consequences of their disobedience. Jesus Christ took our foolishness and nailed it to the cross with His life, and exchanged it with His wisdom. When we accept Him into our lives as

Lord and Savior, we associate with Him, and we will become wise.

King Solomon was the wisest king who ever lived. He prayed for an understanding heart, which is wisdom and insight from God (1Kings 2:7-9). God answered his prayer requests. First Kings 4:30 "Solomon's wisdom excelled the wisdom of all the men of the East and all the wisdom of Egypt." In those days, the countries east of Israel were Persia, Chaldea, and Arabia. The eastern countries and Egypt were powerful empires. They had advanced knowledge of astrology, which gave them supernatural information about the natural world; science; medicine, architecture; astronomy; and geometry. Back then, the Arabs had developed irrigation systems, which brought water to the desert. These empires were intelligent and high in technology at that time. There were also the countries of the Far East like China and India, who were very knowledgeable and intelligent in science and medication. Solomon was wiser than all these ancient civilizations.

Jesus made the universe with His power and wisdom, long before He made humans. Jesus Christ said, "One who is greater than Solomon is here," referring to Himself. (Colossians 1:15-17;

Luke 11:31) If Solomon was wiser than the worldly empires in his day, and Jesus Christ is greater than he is, then we should be the wisest people in the world. First Corinthians 1:30-31 "But of Him you are in Christ Jesus, who became for us wisdom from God…He who glories, let him glory in the LORD." We boast in Jesus Christ and not in ourselves. Godly wisdom is much more powerful than the wisdom of the world, as it gives us insight and discernment into all matters. "Insight" means "the ability to understand the truth about someone or something." Discernment is the ability to judge matters well. The person with godly wisdom is like a bright light. The same way light shines brightly so that those around it will be able to see. You will be someone with wisdom and insight, and therefore, you will be in a position to enlighten many. Jesus Christ said, "Let your light so shine before men, that they may see your good works and glorify your Father in heaven." (Matthew 5:16) This kind of wisdom comes from a relationship with Jesus Christ and knowing the scripture. Godly wisdom surpasses worldly wisdom. Human intelligence and knowledge are shortsighted by human limitation.

Psalm 119:98-100, "You, through Your commandments, make me wiser than my enemies; for they are ever with me. I have more understanding than all my teachers, for Your testimonies are my meditation. I understand more than the ancients because I keep Your precepts." A young person who reads and meditates on the Bible will become wiser than the experts and geniuses of the world. He will even be wiser than more experienced people will, because living by Bible principles becomes his lifestyle, not only for knowledge but to gain wisdom and have a clear direction in his everyday life. Godly wisdom gives us insight into life in general, and it will save us from heartache in the future. Secular education is important and necessary in this world because it opens up opportunities for us, but it has limited wisdom, restricted to its field of study and will give us a financially rewarding career. Someone may be a brilliant architect, but he probably is an alcoholic or has a bad trait of arrogance or greed. On the other hand, the brilliant architect of godly wisdom will be free from any addiction and also be calm and impartial toward others. He will treat his employees fairly and pay good salaries. Godly wisdom will cause the architect to think carefully about the repercussions of any decision he makes. You can get both your secular education and your godly wisdom at the same time.

As we grow in the Lord, our personality will change for better. For example, a businessperson who cheats on his taxes and exploits his employees gives his life to the Lord. He begins to read his Bible and sees Luke 22:21 "...And He said to them, "Render therefore to Caesar the things that are Caesar's, and to God the things that are God's." (Read Romans 13:1-2 and Proverbs 11:1) "Caesar" represents the government. Jesus said that we should keep the rules of the land, which includes paying taxes, obeying traffic laws, and respecting the authority of the relevant government institutions. We may not like certain individuals, but this has nothing to do with them, but with the office they hold. "Render to God the things that are God's" means that our worship to God should take first place in our lives, and we should do His will. The businessperson meditates on this scripture and thinks to himself, "If I want to please God then I must show respect to the government authorities and pay my taxes, and I should treat my employees well by paying them their due, and whenever they work overtime, I will give them the extra payment." He changed from a cheat and greedy man to an honest and fair one. Jesus Christ has this type of effect on a person.

As believers in Jesus Christ, Ralph's daughters stayed away from alcohol and smoking cigarettes because they saw the damage of addiction in their home while growing up. Therefore, they reasoned that if they started to drink alcohol or smoke, there could be the possibility they may become addicted, so they avoided them. Addictions affect a person's health, they are expensive, and they destroy homes. Godly wisdom prevented these young women from making the mistakes of the past. This principle applies to all areas, family life, relationships, finances, and our time, etc. (Read 1 Corinthians 1:20-21, 30) Ralph and Frances' family portray what the ideal best friend should be. Their honest, sincere and compassionate nature, brighten those around them. Relatives, friends, and acquaintances look up to them. This family is the first generation in their lineage to break the curse from off their lives and start the blessings for future generations. By accepting Jesus Christ in their lives, Ralph, Frances, and their daughters allowed Him to transform their lives from being broken due to their dysfunctional family background to stability. Jesus Christ has a positive effect on them so they can now help others to rise higher in life.

Belle's relationship with Jesus Christ has made her into a woman of integrity and virtue. Her transformed life adds value to people she meets by motivating them to rise higher than where they are at present. She uses insight and wisdom to give practical encouragement to them with the appropriate scripture. I am proud to be her friend. Her colleagues respect her because they see the positive effect she has on those she meets. People would like to associate with this type of friend.

Our transformed life is our message to the world. We say more by our lives than with our words. Someone can say anything, but that does not mean he lives up to his words. The way we live, our conduct and mannerism, and our integrity, tells the world who we are. There is a saying, "Action speaks louder than words." With the Holy Spirit in our lives, we would attract hurting people who need help and look for answers. We will have a positive effect on their lives just as our Lord Jesus Christ has on our own. You will get good results when Jesus Christ is your best friend. Jesus blesses us so that we too can become a blessing to others. (Genesis 12:2)

CONCLUSION

To SUMMARIZE, ABUSE IN THE home can break a child severely that his wounds go deep into his subconscious mind and into the center of who he is. It can affect him to the point that he will not know how to handle the simple things in everyday life, like relationships, performing at his job, and making decisions. No matter how maladjusted a person is because of a bad childhood, he should not harbor resentment in his heart toward his abusers. Blaming others and making excuses are futile as they fan the fire of bitterness, which will make him sick. Holding on to past hurts only keep an individual trapped in a prison of misery.

There is a transition period between the present problems and deliverance, which is contentment. Contentment will cause you to enjoy life and be peaceful even though circumstances may be unfavorable. When you accept Jesus Christ in your life, He will heal and deliver you from all injustices ever done to you. Then Jesus will set you free from all negative traits that hold you back from progressing. He will even restore, with interest, all that you lost. You will learn about the authority you have in the name of Jesus Christ to overcome all adversities. Even though you do not like hardships, God uses them to form godly character in you, which makes you into a delightful person.

When Jesus Christ becomes your best friend, He transforms your life from being a broken person to one of wholeness, with an amazing character. People would see you as a source of encouragement and would like to be around you. In turn, you will become the best friend to someone else. You will discover your God-given gift and will get satisfaction from helping others. Just as a light bulb attracts a moth, you would attract people to you without making any effort because of the anointing of the Holy Spirit in your life and your warm disposition. Jesus Christ will free you from every negative quality, hurt, and injustice to someone with a purposeful life. There is no limit to the power of God in your life.

People of good character are outstanding for their high standards. They do not compete with anyone because they are secure in the Lord Jesus Christ.

Reference List

- The Open Bible Expanded Edition, the New King James Version, 1985, Thomas Nelson, Inc.
- Strong's Exhaustive Concordance of the Bible with Hebrew-Chaldee, and Greek Dictionaries, MacDonald Publishing Company, McLean, Virginia 22102, U.S.A.
- Pocket Oxford English Dictionary, Tenth Edition 2005, Clays Ltd., Bungay, Suffolk, Great Britain.
- Iyanla Vanzant, SmileyBooks, Peace from Broken Pieces, How To Get Through What You're Going Through, 250 Park Avenue South, Suite 201, New York, NY 10003, U.S.A., 2010

GLOSSARY

Adhering –   Stick firmly to; follow or observe.

Adversity –   A difficult or unpleasant situation.

Apathetic –   Not interested or enthusiastic.

Debauchery –   Over–indulging in sex, alcohol, and drugs.

Demeanor –   Outward behavior or bearing.

Discretion –   The freedom to decide what should be done in a particular situation.

Eccentric –   An unconventional and rather strange person.

Epitomizes –   Be a perfect example of quality or type.

Harbor –   Keep a thought or feeling secretly in your mind.

Illustration –   An example that proves something or helps to explain it.

Impeccable –	Without faults or mistakes; perfect.
Inadequacies –	Unable to deal with a situation or with life.
Infinity –	The state of being limitless in space or size.
Inherent –	Existing in something as a permanent or essential part or quality.
Introvert –	A quiet person who is mainly concerned with their thoughts and feelings.
Lasciviousness –	Feeling or showing an open or offensive sexual desire
Parenthesis –	A pair of round brackets.
Pleasantries –	An unimportant remark made as part of a polite conversation.
Profusely –	Done or appearing in large quantities; abundant.
Promiscuous –	Having many brief sexual relationships.
Propriety –	Correctness of behavior or morals; the quality of being appropriate.
Relentlessly –	Never stopping or weakening.

Sanhedrin –	The highest court of justice and the supreme council in ancient Jerusalem.
Soothsayer –	A person supposed to be able to foresee the future
Wanton –	Having many sexual partners

BIOGRAPHY

MARIA MARCHAN WAS BORN AND bred on the beautiful twin islands of Trinidad and Tobago in July 1963. She was the first of three children. She grew up in a God-fearing family where regular religious devotions and church attendance were encouraged. Maria's yearning for a deeper level of spirituality and a closer relationship with God evolved into deeper involvement in church life. Her love for the Bible is evident as she finds great pleasure in reading, studying and sharing scripture verses with family, friends, and others; which has become a source of enlightenment, encouragement, and support for many.

From an early age, Maria showed an ability to inspire, empathize and connect with people. Her devotion to children emerged during her childhood. Maria, being the first child and maternal grandchild, often assisted with the daily caregiving of her younger siblings and family members during family gatherings. They all looked up to her. Up to this day, she often engages the elders of her family, community, and workplace in deep conversation, listening and sharing; habitually lending an ear. Maria is the thread that keeps the family connected as she frequently telephones, visits or makes use of social media to maintain regular communication.

She has had her share of challenges as well. Her father, who was an alcoholic, was unable to keep a job. This unstable situation put a strain on the whole family, and although, by all appearances, Maria was growing up in a nuclear family, her mother emerged the main financial, spiritual and emotional supporter of the family. Through her Bible studies, Maria learned and believed that God was able to deliver her father from his addiction. She shared this information with her parents, and they agreed that, as a family, they would pray for him. With persistent prayer and declaring scripture in his life, for example, "I can do all things through Christ who strengthens me," Maria's father eventually gave up alcohol. Owing to this breakthrough, her entire family accepted Jesus Christ as their Lord and Savior. Maria's father became an avid follower of Christ and meditating on the words of the Bible became part of his daily routine. He died twenty years later.

Maria has also had to deal with divorce and the sudden and unexpected deaths of her siblings. Her brother died at the age of twenty-four years old, approximately twenty-seven years ago. Even though the family rallied together, this was a very difficult time for them. During this time of grief, Maria met a young man who appeared to be very supportive. They got married one year after. However, not long after he showed his "true colors." He no longer feigned his interest in Bible studies or in living a life pleasing to God. He did not share her values. According to Maria, "He turned out to be a wolf in sheep's clothing." Maria longed to have children but owing to the rocky and stressful marriage no children were born to this union, which eventually ended in divorce. More recently, she had to deal with the death of her youngest sibling. In the midst of these difficulties, she remained faithful to God, and her relationship with Him grew stronger and stronger.

Maria is fascinated with nature and enjoys the peace and beauty of God's creations, especially mountains, trees, flowers, and rivers. She looks forward to hiking or spending time in her beautiful garden.

Her love for people is only surpassed by her love for the Word of God, which is expressed and shared freely not only in her interactions but her writing as well. She is the author of "The Best Friend." I wait with expectant faith and look forward to reading more of her inspirational work.

Luscia Kanneh

Clinical Psychologist

The New King James Study Bible (1988) Philippians 4:13.

Printed in the United States
By Bookmasters